SOCCER

COACHING by Bill Thomson

METHODS

Soccer Publications, Inc.
3530 Greer Road
Palo Alto, California 94303

ACKNOWLEDGEMENTS

This book goes back a long way—from the initial collection of notes for my own reference to the first attempts at producing written material for coaches. I would, therefore, be remiss if I did not acknowledge some of the people who have assisted me along the way.

Stu Shipp and Brian McVeigh spent considerable time while students at Upper Canada College in demonstrating and photographing skills. In a professional capacity the editorial assistance of Hal Lockwood was much appreciated. I hope that the book will prove a useful source of information for coaches in years to come.

Bill Thomson

Photo Credits

Page 55   Eissner
Page 121   VSW

Printed in the United States of America
Library of Congress Catalog Number 77-86514
ISBN: 0-943752-02-7

CONTENTS

KEY TO DIAGRAMS

SYMBOLS

○ ●	Players of opposing teams
⟶	Direction of ball
----→	Direction of player
∿∿∿→	Player running with the ball
⊕	Ball

POSITIONS

G	Goalkeeper
RB	Right Full Back
LB	Left Full Back
RH	Right Half Back
CH	Centre Half Back
LH	Left Half Back
OR	Outside Right
IR	Inside Right
CF	Centre Forward
IL	Inside Left
OL	Outside Left

Bill Thomson is presently the Director of Coaching of The Canadian Soccer Association. He is a former physical education teacher who graduated from the Scottish School of Physical Education and obtained the full coaching awards of both the Scottish and English Football (Soccer) Associations prior to coming to teach at Upper Canada College in Toronto in 1967.

While teaching at Upper Canada College he graduated with a B.Ed. from the University of Toronto and an MA in Physical Education from the University of Western Ontario.

In 1969 he was appointed part-time Director of Coaching of the Canadian Soccer Association and in 1974 left teaching to take up a full-time position with the Canadian Soccer Association. He is presently reponsible for the implementation of the National Certification program in all Canadian provinces and his duties include conducting coaching clinics for adults and youngsters at all levels of ability.

As team manager of the Canadian National team in the 1975 Pan Am Games and the 1976 Olympic Team, and with his extensive background as a coach and teacher, he brings a wealth of ideas and methods to this coaching manual.

1
COACHING METHODS

COACHING METHODS

The aim of this book is to aid teachers who are introducing soccer into the physical education curriculum, as well as to guide youth soccer coaches who wish to improve their presentations. The novice coach, often lacking the same background or insight into the game as an experienced one, needs to have the basic techniques outlined. To this end techniques are illustrated and accompanied by detailed recommendations for effective coaching.

Many teachers and coaches find they must introduce the game within a limited period of time, and face the problem of achieving optimum development as efficiently as possible. This problem crops up in academic institutions—at all levels—that only allot a limited number of periods to activities such as soccer. Each teacher has to decide whether to spend the time practicing basic skills or practicing the game.

The heart of the matter is that we are dealing with a game comparatively new to this country, in the sense that athletes are unfamiliar with the skills and patterns of play. In North America, games have a basic similarity. In hockey, softball, lacrosse, basketball, tennis, squash, badminton, and even football, the predominate feature is hand and eye coordination. Just as Europeans have concentrated on soccer to the comparative exclusion of other games, we have neglected the coordination skills of soccer in favor of other sports. In most of our games, the feet, and lower limbs in general, have been used only for locomotion, power, direction and positioning after, or during, another skill. This, of course, also applies to soccer, but the important difference is that for the first time we are introducing a factor of control or *skill* to the lower limb area.

The debate between skill coaching and technique coaching has been topical in sports for many years. The difference in approach arises from disagreement over what constitutes skill in the game. Technique coaching is teaching fundamental techniques in isolation from the game (e.g., the push pass in pairs), with no opposition in the practice of them. Skill coaching is approached by setting up situations which involve opponents, supporting players and a target. For example, passing practice of three players against one, with a target of three consecutive passes. These approaches need not be at odds with each other. The danger lies in using one approach exclusively: *only* teaching techniques or *only* using skill drills. The skill approach does not exclude technique practices, but utilizes them to a limited extent.

A skill practice allows the coach to consider the nature of mistakes being made in play. If he determines that they stem from lack of fundamental ability, he will spend some time on the technique involved. However, if he concludes that they are of a decision-making nature and that the techniques are sound, he will continue to expose the player to situations which challenge the execution of his ability. The opposition can be restrained in terms of distance from the player, giving him more time to make the correct decision. Once proficient, the player can be exposed to an unrestrained practice.

A number of considerations must be recognized when coaching or introducing a skill. These can be grouped generally as organization, observation and instruction.

ORGANIZATION

In school, as part of a normal class, the physical education teacher may attempt teaching soccer for a month in the fall or spring. He will be fortunate if he can devote two 40-minute periods per week to it. Problems with facilities and the number of players will encroach on coaching time, forcing the coach to organize and devise a program which takes all these factors into account.

The age group and the level of skill will be further factors which the coach will have to account for. The older age groups, and even semi-pro players who train once or twice a week, stress conditioning, with any skill practice taking the form of a modified indoor game. This approach is sound, since the major weakness is often fitness, but the means to this end are often unrealistic and nonfunctional. For example, the emphasis tends to fall on calisthenics or Swedish drill, which is often badly misused and even harmful. If possible—and here again we must take facilities into account—fitness can be maintained through functional exercises with the ball, pressure training and circuit training. With younger players, on the other hand, time is often best spent on game skills, small-sided games and practices, which run the gamut of skills while producing as much variety and interest as possible. Formal conditioning can be omitted, since skill is the major consideration, and skill practices will give sufficient conditioning to this age group.

Teachers and coaches often find themselves faced with large groups, and limited facilities and equipment. The physical education teacher in particular often faces as many as 40 pupils in a confined gymnasium or on a soccer field, but it is unlikely he will have sufficient equipment for a ratio of one ball to two boys.

Whether faced with training in a gymnasium or on a playground, parking lot or field, the approach should be the same. First, assess the space available with a view to the numbers you have to work with. Second, arrange the class around the best possible practice space so that everyone will be able to see and hear you. The formation will depend on numbers, space and type of practice.

Organization and preparation are essential to good teaching, particularly in physical education, since the nature and diversity of activities require more freedom of movement. Yet activities must be controlled in such a way that a learning, rather than a playing, process can take place.

ORGANIZATION OF THE COACHING SESSION

An excellent coaching aid for organizing and practicing small-sided games is the Coaching Grid, an area marked off in boxes 10 to 20 yards square. Available markings and colored lines in gymnasiums or outdoor practice areas defined by flags, spare balls, shirts, etc., will also do.

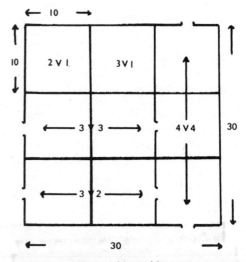

The coaching grid.

The advantages of this organization are:
1. Players have more contact with ball in a small-sided game than they would have playing 11 v 11.
2. The coach has closer contact with the group in a confined area.
3. Large numbers can be controlled better in the grids.
4. The size of the area and the size of the group may be varied in order to practice different aspects of the game.

OBSERVATION

The level of ability of the class or team should be assessed as early as possible, otherwise we may coach above or below their requirements. This may be facilitated by playing a short warm-up game at the beginning of the session. It can be either a normal game or one adapted to focus on specific aspects of play (for example, two-touch soccer will highlight the ability or inability to receive, control and pass quickly). Base your further coaching on what you observe. Pick out a major fault—it may be inaccurate passing—and strive to correct it by practice and experience in passing situations. Even if you have a prearranged theme, a short game is still valuable, apart from the warm up effect, because you can stop and illustrate the skill at the moment the fault occurs by taking it out of the game into the practice situation, then back into the game again, to check improvement. In this way, the practice becomes meaningful and important to the players, rather than something they do before they are allowed to play a game.

Assessment—Involve individual players in some form of realistic situation (see the figure at right—five a side in half field) to allow you to focus on a particular technique.

By making an example of a poor technique, you can illustrate the correct solution and help the players recognize its importance in the game. You should encourage them to analyze the situation themselves. Ask why the play broke down, what the outcome should have been, and how they would correct it.

INSTRUCTION

Technique Practice—If the coach thinks players need to practice a basic technique, it should be isolated from the realistic situation and practiced in groups of three.

This type of practice requires only a short amount of time, as players should quickly

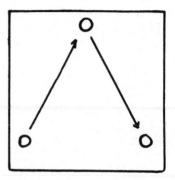

Practice receiving inside of the foot in a triangular formation. Sequence is throw, receive and pass.

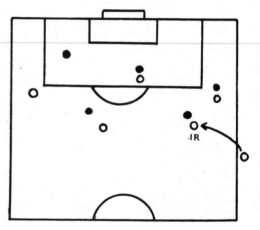

Receiving a throw in, the IR allows the ball to roll under his foot.

become proficient enough to handle a more realistic practice.

Skill Practice—The player should now be exposed to skill practices (see the figure at right). If opposition is introduced into technique practice, work within a confined area. The opponent can be controlled by making him start each practice in the far corner of that area. When the ball is passed, he will try to intercept the ball, but the receiving player will have much more time to receive and decide who to pass to than if the opponent were right on him.

A simple target is three or five consecutive passes; then set up the situation again and repeat. Once the receiving player gains confidence, the opposition can be moved closer and into more realistic covering positions.

Realistic Practice—The coach should make the practice as realistic as possible, in terms of the player's role in the game.

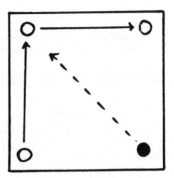

Skill practice with opposition.

Coached Game—Building on this realistic practice, the coach can introduce other groups of players for a normal even-sided game, i.e., forwards against defense, or five a side. Impose limitations on the game to promote certain skills. To give attention to an individual, for example, start by serving him the ball, or use a general game condition such as two-touch soccer (only allowed to touch the ball twice in succession) so that all players are under pressure to receive and pass quickly.

This basic outline applies to most coaching situations, but it is not necessarily a hard and fast scheme. Coaches may adapt it to the time available and group's level of ability.

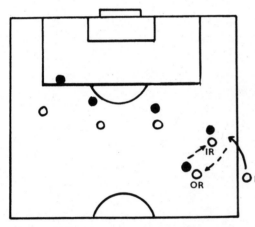

Throw in practice: making space to receive the ball safely and to penetrate. Here the IR and OR have changed positions quickly, leaving the RH to make a selection.

Although it is virtually impossible to remember each point when actually coaching, the preparation and critical examination of each coaching theme is the important thing.

2
PASSING AND SHOOTING

In North America, soccer is generally described as the game where players kick a ball around the field.

Although fundamentally true, this idea suggests a lack of purpose and accuracy. The soccer coach must emphasize the difference between just kicking the ball and kicking it accurately. There are occasions in the game when players under pressure give little thought to accuracy, but generally the purpose of kicking the ball is to pass to a teammate or to shoot at goal.

Inaccurate passing and shooting represent the greatest weaknesses of combined team play. While accuracy is necessary in both passing and shooting, there is an essential difference. A good pass is one that can be played first time by the receiver (i.e., accurate and not too hard). Conversely, a good shot is one that cannot be played or stopped by the prospective receiver, namely, the goalkeeper.

The following illustrations are included for the benefit of the beginning coach, who may not be familiar with the various techniques of striking the ball. Some typical applications of each technique are mentioned together with coaching points.

TECHNIQUES

Inside Of Foot Pass

• To pass accurately

COACHING POINTS

1. Contact centre of ball with flat surface of inside of foot
2. Accelerate lower leg on contact
3. Follow through after contact

Outside Of Foot Pass

- To pass without breaking running stride
- To pass to the side
- To curve the path of the ball

COACHING POINTS

1. Position at side of ball
2. Contact with outer edge of foot—"toe in"
3. Follow through

Low Drive

- To pass over longer distance
- To shoot at goal

COACHING POINTS

1. Step up to the ball
2. Contact with instep (on the laces of the boot) toe down, knee over the ball
3. Snap lower leg quickly
4. Follow through after the ball

Lofted Pass

- To lift the ball over a defender to pass
- To shoot high at goal

COACHING POINTS

1. Approach the ball at an angle
2. Long last stride to the ball
3. Supporting foot to the side and behind the ball
4. Long free leg swing, straightening on contact
5. Contact ball with inside of instep and firm ankle
6. Lean back to lift the ball

Chip Pass

- To lift the ball sharply over opponents for passing or shooting

COACHING POINTS

In a chip shot the ball should rise quickly and sharply. The technique is the same as the lofted pass technique except that the weight and body position should be more over the ball and the contact should be lower and sharper. Extend the lower leg quickly, with the foot stabbing like a golf wedge. This motion will give greater height over less distance.

Swerving The Ball

- To curve the ball around opponents in shooting and passing

COACHING POINTS

1. To spin ball toward body, contact with instep to right of centre
2. To spin ball away from body, contact with outside of foot to left of centre

The Low Volley

- To shoot powerfully
- To clear the ball from defence

COACHING POINTS

1. Judge flight of ball
2. Adopt balanced position
3. Contact with instep, (laces) toe down
4. Follow through in direction of ball

The Short Volley

• To make short pass without ball touching ground

COACHING POINTS

1. Watch ball as it drops
2. Assume balanced position on one foot, with free leg raised and ready to contact
3. Quick contact on instep or inside of foot, with short swing from the lower leg

The Half Volley

• To shoot on goal
• To clear the ball

COACHING POINTS

1. Judge bounce of the ball—step in to contact as it touches ground
2. Contact over the ball with instep or inside of foot
3. Swing and follow through as it touches ground

The Side Volley

- To shoot powerfully
- To clear the ball from defence

COACHING POINTS

1. Exaggerate balanced position by leaning back and to side of ball
2. Allow long, powerful leg swing
3. Point opposite shoulder at target to obtain full power

The Overhead Volley

- To make surprise shot with back to goal
- To make desperate clearance from defender

COACHING POINTS

1. Judge "drop" of ball
2. Lean back to allow leg to straighten and swing
3. "Scissor" jump to change legs
4. Contact as high as possible with firm instep, follow through and fall backwards

PASSING AND SHOOTING PRACTICES

The grid system should be used as much as possible to develop passing and shooting skills in realistic practices. With younger or inexperienced players, however, some time might have to be devoted to the techniques of contacting the ball, in order to perfect inside and outside of the foot passes, chips and volleys. It is pointless to call for a certain type of pass in a practice if the player has not mastered the basic technique. If other factors, such as opposition and targets, are set up too early, the technique and, therefore, the skill factor will break down. If at any time a practice breaks down due to poor technique, this is obviously the moment to run a simpler practice stressing that point.

Following the outline proposed under COACHING METHODS, the practices described below can be used. The coach should determine whether their needs are of a technique or decision-making nature and select drills pertinent to his players' stage of development.

Technique Practice

A variety of formations are used for technique practices. For example, all of the techniques can be practiced individually against any rebound surface (wall or hockey boards) and, if facilities permit, there are definite advantages to this method.

Individual Practice

1. Practice rebounding the ball off the wall from a distance of 5–10 yards using various techniques, e.g., inside and outside of foot.

2. Instep drive
   a) Teach instep contact by leaning against the wall with the ball a few inches away. Practice jamming the ball against the wall with the instep (coaching points) to get the feel of the contact.
   b) Practice instep drive by pushing ball against wall from a distance of 10 yards and then driving the rebound with the instep. Body position will determine the flight of the ball.

3. The techniques of chipping or lofting the ball can be taught by adjusting body position and contact with the ball. A beginner will find it easier to lift a ball by chipping or lofting if the ball is rolling towards him. He can get his contact foot under the ball better as it rolls up than by kicking a stationary ball.

4. Wall passing—running alongside a rebound wall, passing and receiving the ball with the inside and outside of foot.

Pairs Practice

Practices designed for a rebound wall can also be done in pairs. Most coaches would rather work in threes in order to encourage players not to pass back to the same player. However, working in pairs is often easier to organize in a gymnasium and gives players more contact with the ball.

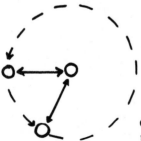

One player runs in a circle while the other player passes first time using various methods.

One player changes his position by moving in and out in order to vary the weight and method of passing, depending on the distance.

INTERPASSING AND SHOOTING ACTIVITIES

No Goalkeeper

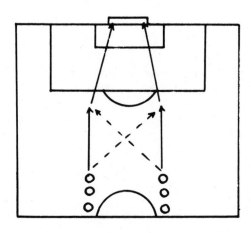

Two players 20 yards apart, interpassing and finishing with a shot from edge of penalty area.

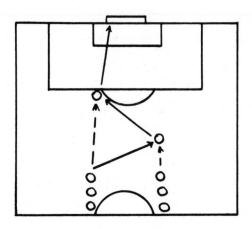

Each player starts with a ball, makes a forward pass and crosses over to shoot partner's ball.

Wall Pass

One player passes from 5 yards away and receiver "rebounds" the ball with the inside of his foot just ahead of his teammate.

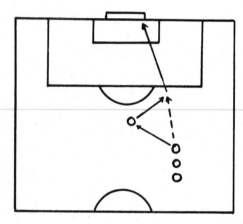

The same movement as above in front of a real or makeshift goal, finishing with a shot.

In Threes and Larger Groups
Shuttle Runs

A passes to B and follows the ball to take B's place as he passes to C. Repeat.

A passes to B, who passes back to A on the move, who gives a wall pass to B on the move.

Triangular Formations

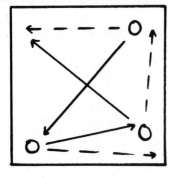

Passing and moving to a new position within a ten-yard square.

Man in the Middle

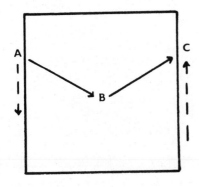

B receives pass from A and turns to pass to C moving along line.

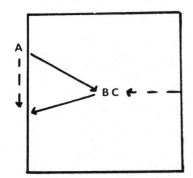

As B receives ball, C attempts to intercept or tackle. Therefore, B must be aware of position of C. Coach A to call "man on," if C is challenging, or "turn," if B is in the clear.

SKILL PRACTICES

Passing and shooting are best taught in "live" situations. The following practices are intended for confined areas, boxes or grids marked out with corner flags, balls, etc., on or off the field of play. Dimensions can range from 10 to 20 yards square to suit varying ability levels.

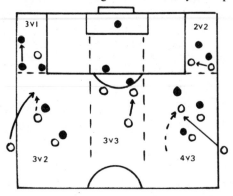

The practices are 3 v 1, 4 v 2, 3 v 2, 2 v 1, 3 v 3, 3 v 4, 5 v 5, and 7 v 5. These practices are competitive—the target being possession and the theme being constant movement.

3 v 1 Situations

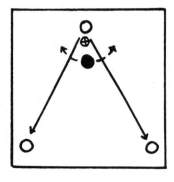

This is a fairly easy situation, in which the players can develop a feel for the various types of contact. The target is possession and number of passes with the ball (3 or 6 passes without interception).

COACHING POINT

Stress running off the ball to give more alternatives to man on the ball

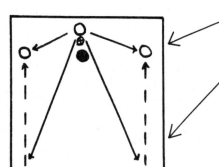

Less space and time but good support and pass angles.

More space and time but poor passing angles.

COACHING POINTS

1. Players will naturally assume a triangular formation with little movement to receive the ball
2. Players will have to be taught how to move intelligently to give support to the man with the ball

Pass and Move or Give and Go

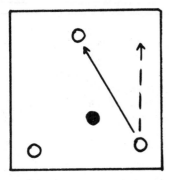

Make the pass, then follow the ball to give support to the receiver.

COACHING POINT

Man on ball points where he wants teammate

Blind Side Running and Cutting

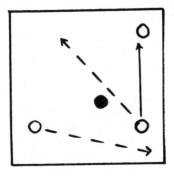

Pass, then cut across defender's path without obstructing, while other teammate runs on his "blind" side to create new passing alternative.

Square Passing

If the target is changed to that of reaching a corner of the confined area or a specific side of the box, then the defender will tend to leave the ball carrier and cover space more. Therefore, this is an ideal situation for finding out ways to get past him without lying behind him (offside).

Receiver (A) draws defender to him or moves in front to collect ball and sends a square pass to B. If defender moves across to intercept, then B would square pass back to A. If the feeder (C) follows his pass, then he can create another alternative square pass from A on his left (overlap).

Target Line

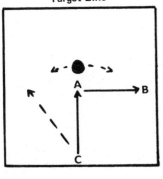

Wall Passing

Target Line

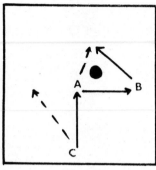

In this instance A uses B as a wall to collect a return pass on the run as the defender is turning. If feeder (C) moves up quickly, then A has an alternative of wall passing on either side (overlap).

Setting Up Pass

Target Line

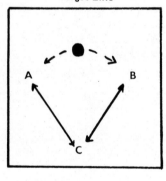

Feeder (C) probes the defender's movements by playing the ball back and forth to A and B. They are setting up the situation to determine what kind of pass is "on," depending on the movement of the defender (i.e., to the receiver or to the space, in anticipation of another pass).

Target Line

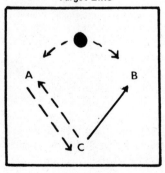

Triangular running and change of position are also effective here. Feeder passes, then runs, to become a receiver, while the receiver takes the feeder's position.

Through Pass

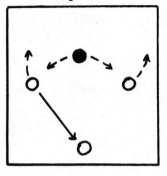

Target Line

From a setting up play, both receivers can break for a through ball. The feeder selects the most penetrating pass.

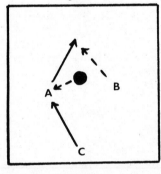

Target Line

C up to A, who sends the ball through to B on the run.

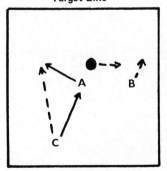

Target Line

C up to A, who fakes pass to B and sends through ball to overlapping feeder (C).

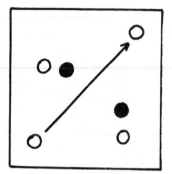

4 v 2

This situation is still an overloaded situation but, because of the confined area, the need to use square, setting up, through and wall passes, together with purposeful running, becomes apparent.

The target in this practice, apart from possession, is getting a through ball between the defenders—trying to catch them lying square (in line) in order to play through a space.

Wall Pass

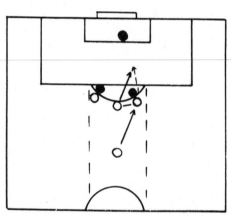

On the other hand, if the defenders are confined to the D of the penalty box, the alternative would be to release an attacker past them into the box.

The attackers force a defender to commit himself by playing the ball to a marked man, who then effects a wall pass by passing the ball off first time.

Setting Up Play

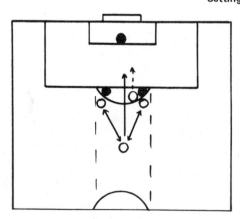

By playing the ball in and back, the attackers can spread the defenders, leaving openings for a through pass.

SHOOTING PRACTICES

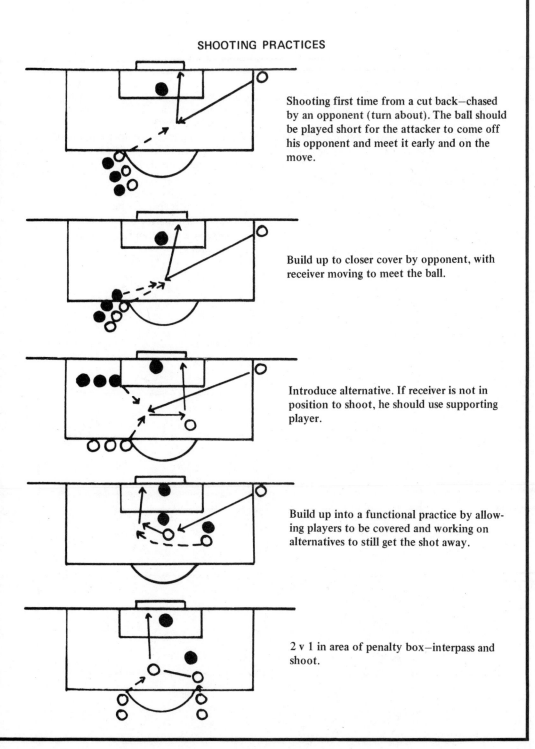

Shooting first time from a cut back—chased by an opponent (turn about). The ball should be played short for the attacker to come off his opponent and meet it early and on the move.

Build up to closer cover by opponent, with receiver moving to meet the ball.

Introduce alternative. If receiver is not in position to shoot, he should use supporting player.

Build up into a functional practice by allowing players to be covered and working on alternatives to still get the shot away.

2 v 1 in area of penalty box—interpass and shoot.

3 v 2 and 2 v 1

This situation is even closer to a game situation. In a game, this type of overloading is common on a fast attacking break. Resistance is easier for the defending players than the attack is for the offensive players, since they can close space more easily and it is difficult for the attackers to offer alternatives to the man in possession. Constant movement by the players off the ball is highlighted in this practice, in which all the interpassing techniques covered earlier are relevant.

In tighter situations, the individual skill of the ball carrier—in screening, faking and ball control—becomes crucial in terms of the time supporting players have to change position and show themselves to the ball. Passing opportunities in this situation come and go in a split second. Quick reactions are of the utmost importance. These situations provide match conditions, and players can practice in the groupings they are likely to encounter on the field

Build up into a full game situation by introducing new players from time to time. This will make circumstances more realistic and present more opportunities for passes and interceptions.

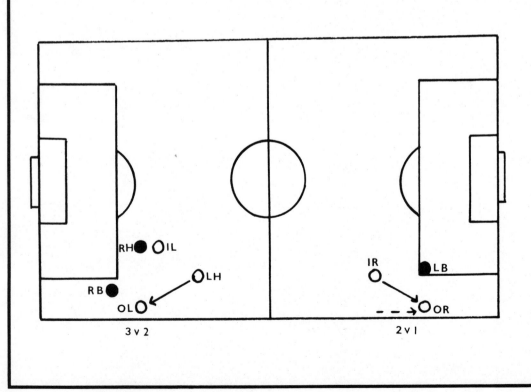

3 v 2

2 v I

ATTACKING BUILD UP

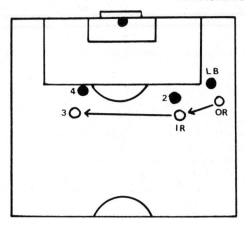

Play starts with a basic 2 v 1 situation (1) on the right wing. After success in this skill we can introduce an opposing halfback (2) to cover IR. This becomes more difficult so we add a third forward (3) on the left wing—open for the switch of play. Then he will be covered (4) and in this way we add players offering alternatives and defenders providing cover until we build up a full game situation. The practice promotes interpassing skills and familiarizes players with switching the point of attack.

3 v 3

More realistic situation—man for man marking. Expand the zones and set up targets building up to 4 v 4 and 5 v 5. Still stressing the passing techniques, look also for the long ball into attack and zoning on the ball to create known situations, e.g., 2 v 1.

Ball is passed to OR, and IR moves across to create a 2 v 1 situation.

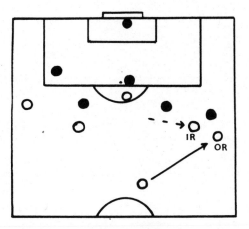

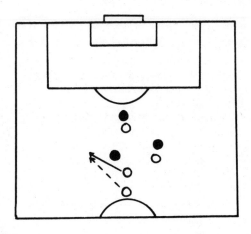

3 v 4

An extension of 3 v 3, this practice features a seventh man who joins the side which has possession, always creating an overload of players attempting to take advantage of the extra man by overloading the situation.

5 v 5 and 7 v 5

Build up to forwards v defence by introducing two halfbacks to feed the forwards. This simulates a real game situation. Concentrate on intelligent build up of midfield with quick zoning and over-loading of the defence when the fast break is "on" in order to take advantage of the situation and produce a scoring opportunity.

In this situation various combinations of smaller situations and longer passing switch plays can be practiced in a realistic game situation. These passing combinations can be practiced using only the players involved initially and then placing them in the game situation.

We are concerned at the moment with passing practices, but this is obviously an excellent opportunity to coach principles of play and tactics of both offense and defence.

Wing Play and "Cut Back" Ball

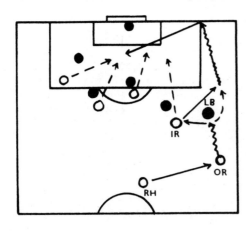

RH feeds the ball to the OR who has come back deep to receive the pass. He carries the ball up to the LB and makes a wall pass with the IR who has come up to support. The OR receives the return pass and goes to the goal line to cut the ball back across the goal area for any of the strikers to run on to and shoot. The ball can be fed left or right, so it is possible to have both wings practicing at the same time with two balls going.

Set Up and Through Ball

LH builds up an attack in midfield by pushing the ball through to the CF who comes to meet the ball, bringing the CH with him, and sets the ball back to the LH who pushes a through ball in for the CF or any other striker cutting in to run on to. If the CH isn't drawn out of position, then the CF has time to collect it, turn, and attempt to run with the ball or wall pass.

Switch of Play

OR, having caused the defence to turn, feeds the ball back to the RH, who switches play with a long cross-field pass to deep-lying OL. He is in a position to collect the ball freely and attempt to wall pass or, in this case, cross a long ball to the far post for strikers, switching play again and catching the defence on the turn.

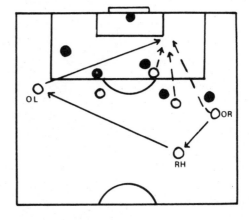

Decoy Runs and Use of Long Ball

OR runs as if to receive pass from the RH, bringing LB out of position. This leaves room for IR or CF to break into space on wing to receive long ball from RH. Decoy running can be used in many instances to create space between and behind defenders.

3
DRIBBLING AND TACKLING

Dribbling is best taught in live situations hand in hand with tackling and interception as both skills are directly in opposition and attackers and defenders can be coached in the same situation.

For the benefit of coaches who may be unfamiliar with dribbling and tackling techniques the following illustrations are examples of conventional methods.

DRIBBLING TECHNIQUES

Inside And Outside Of Foot

• To change direction and avoid an opponent

COACHING POINTS

1. Play ball in a definite direction with inside of foot
2. Quickly step over ball
3. Change direction and pace by moving away quickly, playing ball with outside of foot

SCREENING

• To shield ball from opponent and prevent him from tackling

COACHING POINTS

1. Keep body between ball and opponent without leaning on him (obstruction)
2. Be aware of both ball and opponent
3. Quickly alter position as opponent moves
4. Control techniques: tap ball with inside and outside of foot, roll ball forward and pull it back with sole of foot, holding it at a distance with sole of foot

TACKLING TECHNIQUES

Front Block

• To challenge an opponent from the front

COACHING POINTS

1. Eye on the ball
2. Timing: contact ball with inside of foot as opponent touches it
3. Step into the tackle, weight carried through centre of ball and supported by other leg behind and to side of ball with knees bent

After block contact, follow through by rolling ball over opponent's foot.

After block contact, follow through by forcing ball through opponent's legs to receive on far side.

Side Block

• To challenge an opponent from the side or rear

COACHING POINTS

1. Approach from rear
2. Step in close to ball, supporting foot level with ball
3. Pivot quickly on foot to contact the ball in the front block position

Heel Tackle

• To challenge an opponent moving at speed

COACHING POINTS

1. Approach from rear—eye on ball
2. Lift near leg over ball, blocking it with the heel
3. Follow through to recover ball, turning to control the ball

Slide Block

• To dispossess opponent from the rear

COACHING POINTS

1. Approach as close as possible
2. Fold inside leg and go down on side, breaking fall with hand and arm
3. Swing outside leg around to contact ball with instep in a block position

Hook Slide

- Approach from the rear and slide the ball out of an opponent's possession in a dangerous situation

COACHING POINTS

1. Approach as close as possible
2. Take off on outside leg, sliding down on inside arm and side
3. Slide inside leg around to hook ball away with instep before opponent touches it again

Split Slide

- To dispossess a dangerous opponent from the side

COACHING POINTS

1. Close approach from side
2. Fold front leg, breaking fall with one arm and sliding rear leg forward to contact ball with sole of foot

TECHNIQUES OF RUNNING WITH THE BALL

Initially, players should be allowed to run with the ball to familiarize themselves with the techniques. Some of the techniques that should be introduced through these practices are:

1. Running with the ball close to the feet—outside and inside
2. Running with the ball varying pace: stop, go, sprint, jog, etc.
3. Weaving rhythms using inside and outside of foot
4. Swerving with or without playing the ball
5. Twisting and turning with the ball in a confined space

Although valuable for improving ball control, technique practices should not be overemphasized. Skill practices are more worthwhile.

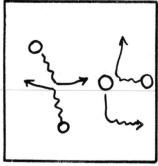

Using a ten-yard grid or confined area, players move about feinting, dodging and swerving to avoid contact with another ball or player.

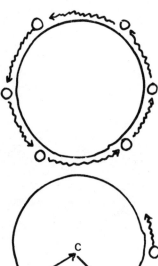

Run with ball around centre circle, changing direction on command. Techniques:

1. Use outside of foot when running freely with ball—allows a full stride.
2. When changing direction, stop ball with sole of foot and roll it back in the opposite direction without losing sight of it.

Run with ball as above, but look up for signal from coach in centre pointing (not calling) for the ball. Player makes a push pass to coach and runs around player in front to receive return pass and continue running with the ball. Repeat with other players.

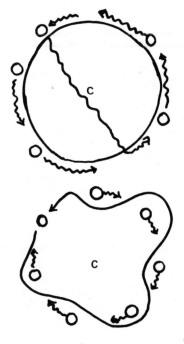

Running as before, player sprints on signal across circle with the ball and drops into line on the far side. Continue as before. Repeat rapidly with other players.

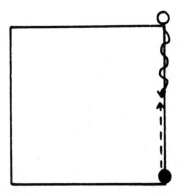

Running as above, player turns on signal, weaving in and out between advancing players until he returns to his place and drops back into line.

Numerous weaving and shuttle relays can be devised that incorporate techniques of running with the ball.

TACKLING TECHNIQUES

Teach tackling "live." In live situations players learn to time their challenge. Anticipation, jockeying and feinting are the keys to getting within striking distance of the ball. However, beginners initially need practices stressing safe and legal tackling techniques due to the influence in North America of the checking used in ice hockey and the blocking used in football.

The Front Block

Using the grid lines or any suitable marking, have one player carry the ball down the line toward a defender. The defender attempts to keep forward on his toes, feinting a tackle. If the ball carrier loses control, the defender can intercept the ball and take it back to his end of the line. If the forward keeps close control then the defender times his contact for a front block tackle. The attacker can anticipate this and, once the initial contact is made, both players attempt to get possession of the ball and reach the other end of the line before being tackled again.

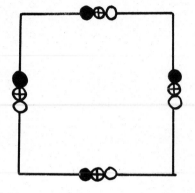

Methods of winning the ball after contact can be practiced by having players assume the contact position of the front block tackle. When the coach signals, they attempt to win the ball by pushing it through opponent's legs or rolling it over his foot to reach the far end of the line before being tackled again.

Tackling From the Side and Rear

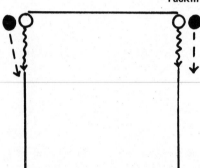

Practice tackling from the side and from behind by having one player try to run down the line to the other end without losing the ball to a defender. The ball carrier will run with the ball and, after the initial contact, will try to regain possession of the ball, a predicament he frequently will face in the game.

By regulating the starting position of the tackler and controlling the speed of the ball carrier, the coach can affect what kind of tackle will be made. The technique to be used will depend upon how close the tackler can get to the ball carrier before he reaches his target. For example, the tackler should catch up to the ball carrier and make an upright block tackle if at all possible. However, if the ball carrier is moving too fast for the tackler to catch up and get around him into a block position, then he may be forced to dispossess him with a slide tackle.

A number of these techniques can be combined by designating targets for the ball carrier and controlling his direction of running with the ball.

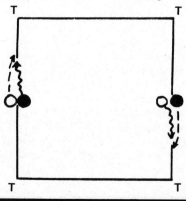

As before, one player approaches with the ball down a line. At contact, both players attempt to win the ball and reach the far end of the line. The losing player must attempt another tackle to regain the ball or slide the ball out of reach before the ball carrier reaches the target (T).

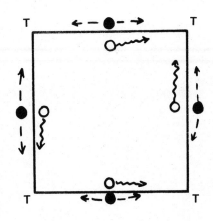

Feinting and screening techniques can be practiced around the grid with defender limited to his side of the line. Target for ball carrier is to reach one end of line. Defender anticipates move of ball carrier and keeps beside him. Later he can be allowed to strike for the ball if it touches the line.

1 v 1 in the Grid

Screening and feinting while running with the ball is practiced with the defender running alongside and attempting to tackle.

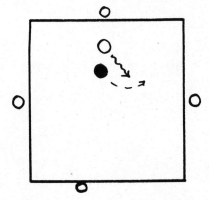

A more realistic practice for both dribbling and tackling is this 1 v 1 situation inside the grid. The target is to reach any side except the one behind the ball carrier. When he succeeds, the supporting player takes over the ball.

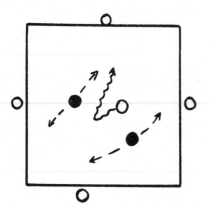

Later, with the introduction of a second defender, all sides can become targets. Tackling principles of support and cover can be coached while ball carrier uses dribbling skills to reach any side.

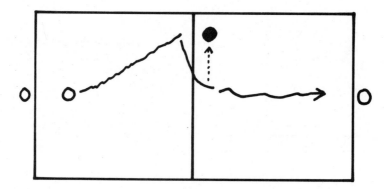

With the ball under control, run against an opponent who is restricted to a line between two grids. Change of pace, swerving, feinting and screening are the skills needed to reach the target zone. Supporting player repeats the drill.

COACHING POINTS

1. Commit the defender by running quickly at him, forcing him back on his heels
2. Commit the defender to one direction rather than run straight at him
3. Change pace or direction—more difficult for defender to check and chase

When To Tackle

Set up skill practices—with opposition, support, target—to illustrate correct responses to certain situations and to drill players in them.

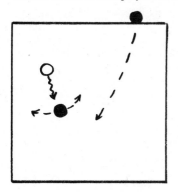

Defender delaying opponent in order to "buy time" for support from the front. Teaches principle of *delay*.

Once support is present in depth (another principle), the defender can attempt to dispossess his attacker. Front block, side tackle and jockeying could be used. Also, in this situation the support coming from the front could do the tackling while the original defender dropped back to cover. This principle, *collective tackling*, is often incorporated into team tactics. If the ball carrier eludes the first challenger, then the supporting player is in a position to challenge.

The coach can make the opponent hold the ball or attempt to beat the man before shooting or dribbling the ball to the end of the grid line, or use other means to control the situation. In the same practice, if the supporting player does not get back in time, the defender is forced to tackle in a 1 v 1 situation if his goal is in danger. If the attacker moves at speed and takes him on, he will have to use one of the preceding methods or, if he moves past him, one of the sliding tackles.

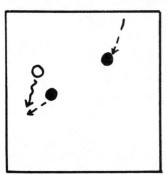

Slide tackle as last resort in dangerous situation. New players can be introduced to create similar but more complex situations.

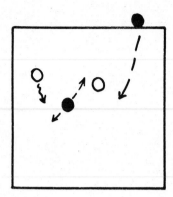

Defender delaying two attackers. He "jockeys" to create interception and "buy time" for returning support. Defender will attempt to prevent inter-passing and to force tackler down the line where there is less space.

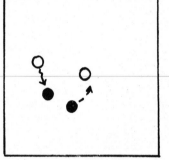

Good balance by rear defender—in good position to cover through ball or close mark other attacker on switch of play.

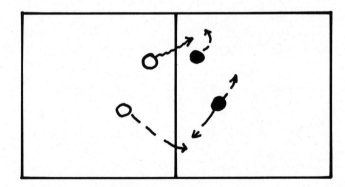

Expand these practices into 2 v 2 across two grids. Coach dribbling, tackling techniques and principles, e.g., attacker needs to commit the defender and draw him into an early attempt, while defender wants to delay and balance before making tackle.

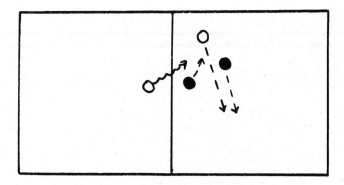

Penetration by dribbling—mobility by free forward destroying cover. Once practices build up to 3 v 3 or five a side, the need to control the conditions becomes apparent. The more passing opportunities, the less dribbling. To make sure players practice dribbling, insist that they beat at least one man before passing or dribbling the ball over the end line.

4
RECEIVING AND BALL CONTROL

The flight or direction of the ball determines the technique used to receive or bring it under control. The following general factors apply:

Movement. Move to a position on the line of flight or direction of the ball in preparation to receive.

Decision. Decide quickly which method to use, but be flexible enough to react to a change of direction.

Preparation. Present the controlling surface and assume a balanced position.

Relaxation. Relax the controlling surface. Give with the ball to bring it under control and move away easily.

With these points in mind, let us look at the specific techniques.

Movement to the Direction of the Ball

• To get into position behind the line of flight of the ball

COACHING POINTS

1. Move quickly to meet the ball
2. Get ready to receive
3. Have some part of the body behind ball to stop progress

CONTROLLING BALL ON THE GROUND

• To bring a ball under control

Sole of Foot

Inside of Foot

COACHING POINTS

1. Judge where ball will drop
2. Contact ball between foot and ground as it touches down
3. Sweep ball away under control

Outside of Foot

CONTROLLING BALL IN THE AIR

• To control a ball in the air before an opponent can intercept

Instep

Inside of Foot

Thigh

Chest (a)

Chest (b)

COACHING POINTS (for controlling ball in the air)

1. Judge drop of ball
2. Relax controlling surface
3. Move off under control

TECHNIQUE PRACTICE

Receiving techniques should be practiced individually before being used in realistic situations. For this reason, juggling or ball familiarity activities are valuable preliminaries. They help players judge the weight and feel of the ball on different parts of the body. Set practices are advised. It is important that players do the set practices exactly as specified, so that they are constantly reacting to the movement of the ball.

INDIVIDUAL PRACTICE

Drop ball from waist height or put sole of foot on ball, roll it back and scoop the ball up with the instep.

1. Play ball with alternate feet, letting it bounce once between contacts.
2. Play ball twice with left foot, twice with right foot and bounce in between.
3. Play ball up to thigh (or drop on to thigh) and keep it in the air.
4. Play ball with foot, thigh, head, thigh, foot, and repeat.

Although juggling improves sensitivity and balance, it is only a means to an end, not an end in itself. More important than keeping the ball up indefinitely is bringing it down. In addition to the juggling practices, coach players to scoop the ball up in the air and then receive it using a variety of techniques. Beginners can, of course, start by simply dropping the ball. When more confident of technique and ability, they can throw the ball higher, as a test of ability.

All of the techniques illustrated here can be practiced in this way. Players can practice in pairs, with one player passing or throwing to the other to sharpen his reactions. He must quickly decide which method to use, and adjust accordingly. The following techniques might be stressed in practice:

1. Receiving a ball approaching on the ground, turning it in various directions using inside and outside of foot, feinting as if to play the ball, and allowing it to run with minimum control.
2. Use of instep, high and low, use of thigh, chest and head to control a dropping ball, or to angle ball in a new direction.
3. Varying services by changing distance, height and speed.
4. Use of sole of foot for receiving ball, for pushing it forward, for trapping high bouncing ball, for trap passing.
5. Use of wedge, with both the inside and outside of foot.

GRID PRACTICES FOR RECEIVING

2 v 1

Server throws ball from far corner, receiver controls and passes to teammate before server can intercept or tackle. In the same situation practices of receiving with thigh, chest and head can be done.

Less Space and Time

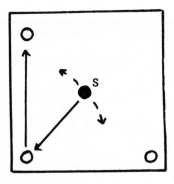

Server (S) throws from the centre of the grid. The receiving player has to react quickly to control the ball. The use of "wedge" passing and screening as ball is controlled become necessary skills.

Receiving on the Turn

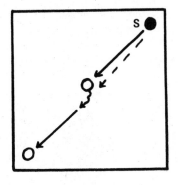

Receiver in center of the grid practices receiving on the turn, left and right, with inside and outside of foot. He makes a pass to man behind or, feinting, lets the ball run past to the man behind. Finally, he receives and screens the ball from server (S) before passing.

Receiving Under Pressure

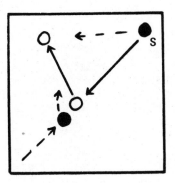

Server (S) throws to marked receiver, who moves forward to control the ball. He quickly passes it off to unmarked teammate before he can be tackled or his pass intercepted.

RESTART PRACTICES

Receiving From a Throw In

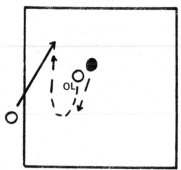

From a throw in, the OL feints to collect the ball and runs down the line.

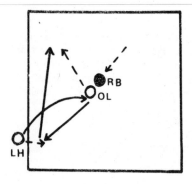

The OL, drawing the RB with him as he moves to receive, trap passes the ball back to the wing half (LH), who passes down the line for him to run on to.

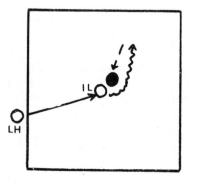

IL runs to receive ball from the LH, but, instead of playing it back first time, turns the ball round his opponent with the outside of his foot, or allows it to roll through his legs and receives it on the run past his opponent.

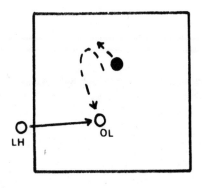

OL fakes collecting the ball on the wing and comes back to take a shorter throw from the LH, creating a 2 v 1 situation against the opposing fullback.

Receiving From a Goalkeeper's Throw or Goal Kick

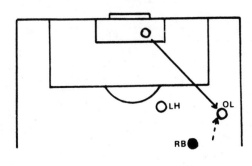

Throw goes to OL coming back deep to collect ball, receiving and playing back to LH, or turning to create 2 v 1 situation on fullback.

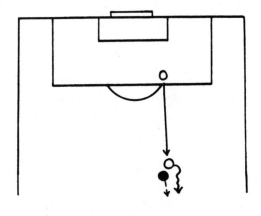

Forward practices collecting and turning with the ball while tightly marked.

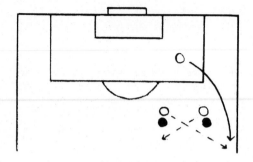

Use of diagonal running and faking to receive ball on the run and make space.

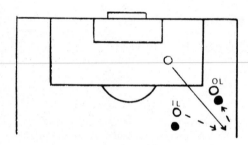

Use of decoy run by OL for IL to collect ball on the move.

Receiving From Corner Kick or Free Kick

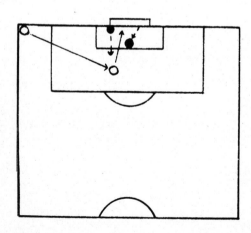

Controlling a hard-hit ball and shooting before being challenged by defender. Restrain defender at goal line.

GAME-RELATED PRACTICES

Players rotate around the field in groups of three. At each station they perform the practices outlined below and change attack and defence roles. The goalkeepers remain in their goal areas at each end.

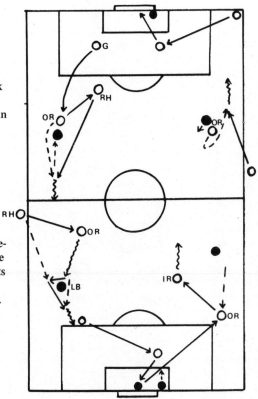

Goalkeeper throws to OR, who plays it back to RH, who receives through ball on the run up the wing to reach halfway line.

OR fakes inside, then receives ball on the run along wing, reaching goal line. Reward is a hard-hit corner received quickly and shot at goal.

Winger leaves LB to receive throw and create 2 v 1 situation. Effects a wall pass to reach target of penalty box. Reward is a hard-hit free kick received quickly and shot at goal.

Quick throw to OR coming back deep. Playing ball off to IR or creating a 2 v 1 situation to reach halfway.

5
HEADING

Heading causes more apprehension than any other technique. The initial fear which most children have of being hit on the head with the ball is understandable, particularly if the ball is heavy or wet. Some children will be quite confident in attacking the ball but may experience pain because of a poor contact. The coach, therefore, should recognize these difficulties when dealing with beginners, or with players who exhibit poor technique in a game situation.

The basic techniques of heading are outlined below.

FACE ON

- To head powerfully at goal
- To clear the ball from defence

COACHING POINTS

1. Assume balanced position facing ball
2. Legs propel trunk and head forward to meet ball
3. Contact flat on forehead above eyes
4. Follow through after contact, directing ball with powerful extension of neck

Heading to Side

- To direct the ball to a teammate
- To head into goal

COACHING POINTS

Same as above, but turn head and neck on contact with ball to redirect it

In the Air

- To contact the ball as high as possible, heading it into the goal or clearing the ball before an opponent is able to intercept

COACHING POINTS

1. Long last stride for one-foot take off
2. Arch back in preparation for contact
3. Contact flat on forehead
4. Follow through with trunk and neck, bringing legs forward to compensate for forward rotation

Initially, a lighter, rubber ball may be used in technique practices to improve confidence.

SOLO HEADING

A tether ball suspended from the crossbar provides an excellent coaching aid for beginners, allowing them to contact the ball on the forehead and head the ball continuously.

The initial feel of the ball can also be experienced simply by throwing the ball up to head and catch. The next step is to head the ball two or three times before losing control.

PAIRS HEADING

The sensation of hitting the ball rather than being hit by it can be produced by practicing in pairs or solo against a wall if a partner is not available. Initially the player can hold the ball with outstretched arms and pull the ball onto his forehead to "fire" it out of his hands. In this way he can concentrate on correct contact and the sensation of striking the ball. The following are effective pair exercises:

1. One player throws underhand and the other heads the ball back to his feet for him to control.

2. One player sits down with legs outstretched and hands off the ground for balance. Partner serves from a few yards away for him to head back powerfully, using neck and trunk action.
3. Heading for power: partner serves from five yards for player to powerfully head the ball back over his head for distance using the neck and trunk action.
4. As before, using single and double foot take off.

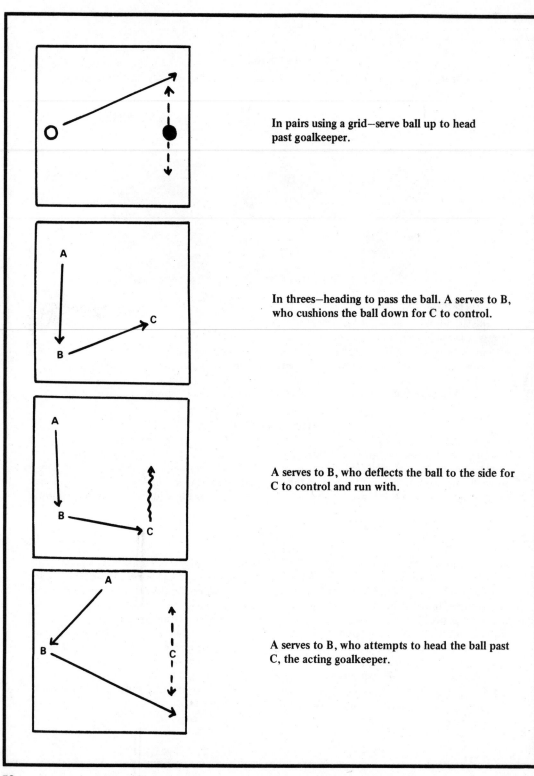

In pairs using a grid—serve ball up to head past goalkeeper.

In threes—heading to pass the ball. A serves to B, who cushions the ball down for C to control.

A serves to B, who deflects the ball to the side for C to control and run with.

A serves to B, who attempts to head the ball past C, the acting goalkeeper.

Having overcome initial fear of contact with the ball, players may have a secondary fear: contact with other players. Many players master the individual techniques but fear to try them in a game because they think they will crash into an opponent while heading the ball. Here again, the coach must build confidence in apprehensive players by gradually exposing them to more realistic situations. Help them recognize what techniques to use under pressure and how to achieve success. Again, the grid system is very suitable. As in other skill situations, the coach can control the closeness of the opponent and, by doing that, the available time as well.

DEFENSIVE HEADING

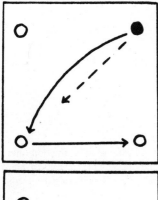

Initial introduction—high service from opponent who immediately becomes challenger. Receiver heads ball to supporting player.

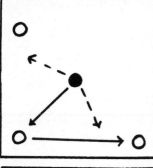

Same situation, but with less space and time. Practice develops players' ability to assess options quickly and to head the ball down powerfully.

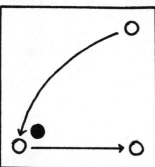

Receiver takes a long service from the far corner, with closer opposition. Practice heading for power —back to server or down to support. Practice take-off—single and double jump.

Restart Practices

Throw In

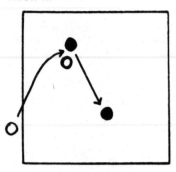

A throw in goes to the forward. The defender, closely marking him, clears the ball by playing it out or to target man, if possible.

Corner and Free Kick

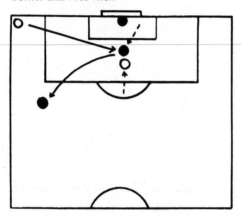

On a corner kick or chip service, the defender heads the ball high, clearing it to support man. Judge run-up and take-off well for good timing and power.

Goalkeeper's Throw or Goal Kick

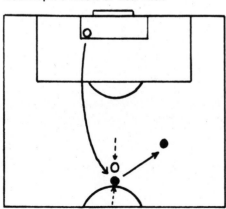

When meeting a throw from the goalkeeper, timing and take-off are very important. Player should meet the ball high and play it down to his support.

ATTACKING HEADING

Attacking involves the same principles as defending or clearing and should be approached in the same way. In fact it is often useful to teach both offensive and defensive strategies for the same situation. Show both offense and defence exactly why they succeeded in that instance or what they have to do to change circumstances and win. Much of the success the attacking team will have in heading practice depends on the service to the receiver.

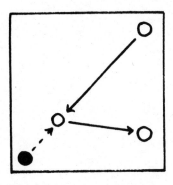

In the same heading situation as the one shown earlier, the offense can turn it to their favour. If it is a low ball played short, for an attacker to come off the defender, he can cushion it and head down to a supporting player. Here the attacker is involved in a typical environment and is shown an acceptable solution. As a consequence, the opponent will mark tighter, but this should not present further problems.

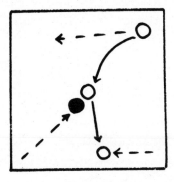

If the service is high, it becomes difficult to play the ball back, so the attacker has to deflect the ball past the defender to on-rushing support. Good judgment of timing and take-off is vital to attackers as well as defenders.

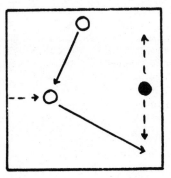

Power heading and diving heading can be introduced to attackers as illustrated—giving them sufficient space and time to make the movement. Once confidence has increased, this space can be closed up.

Restart Practices

Throw In

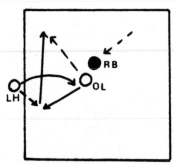

LH throws in to OL, who heads ball back to LH to draw RB forward. OL receives ball on the run from LH.

Goalkeeper's Throw/Kick

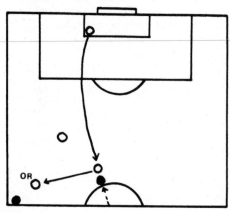

Receiver of goalkeeper's throw/kick heads ball back to support or deflects it to OR.

Corner Kick

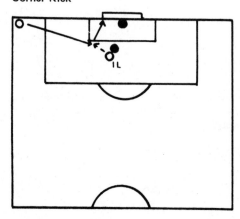

This figure shows power heading for goal from corner kick. Ball should be played short, to near post, so that IL can come off his opponent and meet the ball on the move, arriving late but going at full speed.

These techniques apply to specific situations and, like other techniques, can be effectively practiced in pairs. However, the goalkeeper is not only the last line of defence but the first line of attack (if he gets the ball!). To coordinate his functions properly, he needs realistic play with the rest of the team. One benefit of this kind of practice is that the goalkeeper will save a shot and, without waiting for approval or applause, immediately throw the ball to an unmarked man. He will learn that his skill is a means to a greater end (scoring a goal), rather than an end in itself.

Fielding and Catching

• To gather a low ball by bending closer to it

Down on one knee

COACHING POINTS

1. Get behind line of ball
2. Down on one knee, body behind ball, hands ready
3. Collect ball into pit of stomach and move away quickly

Bending with Straight Legs

COACHING POINTS

1. Get behind line of ball
2. Bend from hips with legs together
3. Collect ball with outstretched hands

6
GOALKEEPING

Falling on Ball

- To stop a shot with the hands when there isn't enough time to get the whole body behind the ball

COACHING POINTS

1. Get down behind the ball by folding body: first legs, then trunk
2. To stop ball, lead with hands and arms
3. Use body as a block to backstop hands and arms
4. After collecting, roll over to protect ball and self, wrapping body tightly around ball

Waist High

- To collect a ball at waist level safely

COACHING POINTS

1. Get into balanced position behind ball, weight forward
2. Have hands and arms ready to receive
3. Collect, and give on impact

Chest and Head High

• To collect a ball at chest or head level

COACHING POINTS

1. Meet ball as early as possible
3. Raise hands towards ball, fingers widespread behind the ball
3. Contact the ball in front of head, give on impact, and bring down to chest

Palming

• To direct ball over the crossbar if unable to collect it or when harassed

Outside Hand   *Inside Hand*

COACHING POINTS

1. Keep eye on the ball, watching the way it drops
2. Take off one foot, swing arms for more lift
3. Contact with palm and fingers as high as possible, to make sure it clears crossbar

Punching

• To clear the ball from the danger area if unable to collect it and when harassed

Both Hands

COACHING POINTS

1. Keep eye on the ball
2. Take off on one foot to meet the ball as high and as early as possible
3. Contact with both fists flat and together—extend arms to follow through and to direct the ball safely away from goal

One Hand

One Hand

COACHING POINTS

1. Time the take-off to meet ball early
2. Swing far hand and arm overarm at ball
3. Contact and follow through. Clear ball in front of body

COACHING POINTS

1. Go up to meet dropping ball
2. Swing outside arm up under ball
3. Contact with back of hand and follow through. Clear ball behind head

Throwing

Javelin

• To throw the ball accurately to a teammate over a short distance

COACHING POINTS

1. Hold ball with two hands while looking for target
2. Take ball back high in one hand and take long stride forward into balanced throwing position
3. Pull ball past head, extending rear leg and rotating trunk
4. Follow through to add power

Round Arm

• To make long range throw

COACHING POINTS

1. Hold ball with two hands while looking for target
2. Rotate body, turning the back in the general direction of throw, and cup the ball in one hand
3. Leading with opposite leg, unwind the trunk and, with a straight arm, release ball at shoulder level

Overarm Bowl

• To make long range throw with higher trajectory in order to clear opponents

COACHING POINTS

1. Sweep ball back, cupped in one hand, and turn body sideways, in line with the direction of throw
2. Step forward into set position, extending rear leg, rotating hips and shoulders
3. With arm completely extended, sweep arm overhead and release ball

FUNCTIONAL PRACTICE

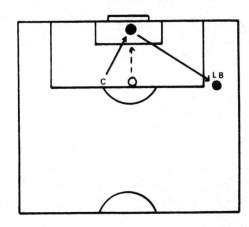

Coach releases opposition (O) after throwing ball to keeper who collects it and throws to fullback (LB).

The coach can feed the ball in different ways to control the practice: evading an opponent and finding a target man with a kick or throw. The opposition challenges the goalkeeper to perform efficiently.

This type of practice will help the coach teach how to narrow the scoring angle and judge when to leave the goal to intercept a through pass or a high cross.

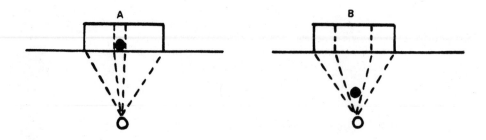

Goalkeeper A, by staying on the goal line, is leaving much more of the goal open than Goalkeeper B, who has narrowed the angle. But the goalkeeper should not come out too far, as this will make it easy to chip the ball over his head. Once again, the coach can give the goalkeeper confidence and experience, while still perfecting technique, by controlling the starting distance and quickness of the opponent.

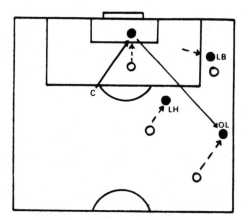

In this practice, the LB is covered, but we may offer other alternatives in the form of a link man (LH) or forward (OL), who have come back to look for the ball.

The goalkeeper's throw or kick starts the attack. A small-sided game can be developed by giving the defence the target of running with the ball (not kicking) past the halfway line. It is important that after each goal the coach starts the game again with a service to the goalkeeper. His onrushing opponent will make him react quickly.

There is one important thing to remember about coaching goalkeepers. It is better to base further skill coaching on observations of the player's performance than on accepted methods. The coach doesn't have to follow them religiously. If a goalkeeper can deal with a situation effectively and safely, the coach should focus his attention on a skill which needs improvement, instead of trying to change an effective style.

To analyze play, and to selectively work on weak skills once they have been recognized, the following challenges might be designed into functional practices:

1. Dealing with an onrushing player who has the ball at his feet.
2. Assessing when to catch a high ball crossed from the wing.
3. Feeding forwards by throwing and kicking.
4. Evading an opponent and throwing to one's own defenders.
5. Methods of taking goal kicks.
6. Positioning when an attacker approaches goal line.
7. Reacting to a succession of shots and deflections.
8. Dealing with high centres against an onrush of opponents.
9. Judging when to come out of goal to pick up a through pass.

7
SYSTEMS AND PRINCIPLES OF PLAY

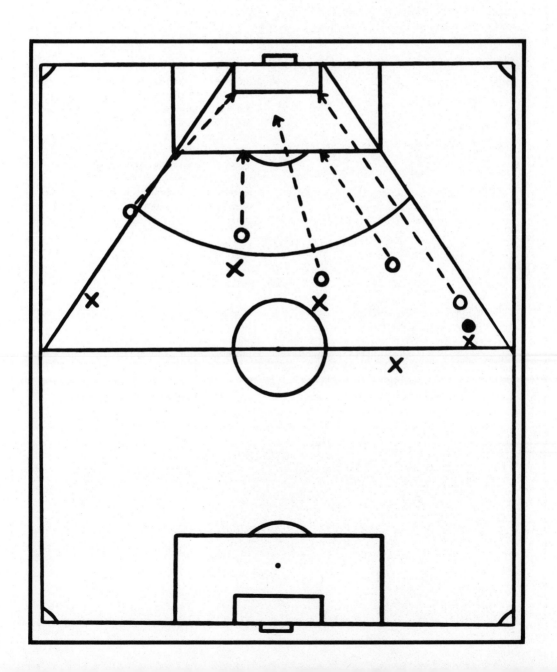

A system of play is simply a method of arranging players on the field in order to carry out particular duties. There are many systems to choose from.

A failing of many coaches is that they impose a popular system on players of different ages, regardless of ability and understanding.

The selection of a particular system of play will depend on a number of factors:

1. The technical ability of the players
2. Their understanding of their part in the game
3. The degree of fitness needed to execute certain systems
4. The system used by the opposing team

The development of a system of play is a recognition of the strategic importance of space. By the specific arrangement of players on the field, coaches close dangerous space when defending and take advantage of open space when attacking. However, it requires a great deal of understanding on the part of players for them to be conscious of these strategies. To simply put them in positions and expect them to emulate a successful system will not help them understand their role in the game.

They need, first, instruction in the basic principles of play. This will also give the coach an opportunity to assess the ability of players in various situations. From this assessment he should evolve a style of play which allows his players to perform to the best of their ability.

It is not necessary that players learn the "labels" which the coach attaches to the principles but simply learn to recognize them and make the required movements intelligently.

ASSESSMENT OF ABILITY AND EVOLUTION OF SYSTEM

The principles of offense and defence are the foundations for the development of systems of play and other tactical considerations. For example, a basic consideration in the game is possession of the ball. In attack, the team must think and act positively, confident and accurate ball control should be stressed and the only justification for loss of possession would be seeing a scoring opportunity, i.e., shooting. Conversely, if possession is lost, the team must think and act defensively and repossession and safety are stressed.

From this basic principle of ball possession, consider the following aspects of attack and defence:

BALL POSSESSION

ATTACK   DEFENCE

ATTACK	DEFENCE
Depth	Depth
Mobility	Balance
Penetration	Delay
Width	Concentration
Improvization	Control/Restraint

ATTACKING PRINCIPLES

Depth in Attack

Intelligent support of the player on the ball will increase the number of passing angles and opportunities. The player off the ball, i.e., not in possession, must support or zone on the ball in order to give support and commit the opposition.

Players should realize to have depth they must have support from behind and not be caught playing square or in a straight line as this will limit their passing opportunities and increase the chance of interception by the opposition.

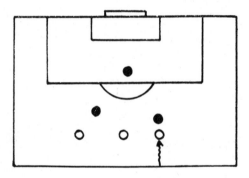

Poor support—no depth! Only square passing possible.

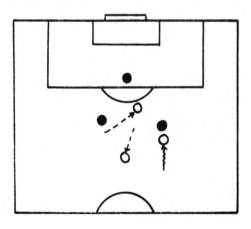

Good support—intelligent running OFF the ball to increase passing opportunities and give depth to attack.

Mobility in Attack

At times, all players, whether in attack or defence, must take on the roles of players around them. If a defender sees an attacker in trouble and moves up to support or overlap, he is showing mobility.

Similarly, an attacking player may have to change position to cover for the overlapping fullback.

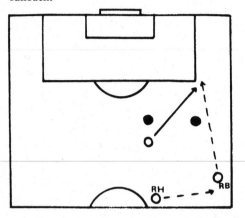

RB goes on overlap run, and RH comes across to support.

Penetration in Attack

Whenever there are two or more passing possibilities the pass which achieves the greatest penetration must be used. The creation of goal scoring opportunities and territorial advantage are the prime objects of penetration.

Assessment:

Waves of attack—how many passes are going between or behind opposition to create scoring opportunities? Or are the attackers keeping possession safely and failing to go for the quick penetrating thrust?

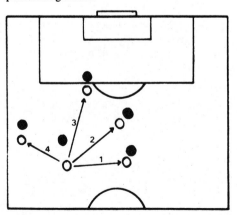

For example, the most penetrating pass in the diagram is obviously No. 3. It goes behind most defenders and creates a 1 v 1 situation which can be overloaded quickly into a 2 v 1 situation for the attack.

Width in Attack

Width in attack should stretch the opposing defence. This will provide open space and, therefore, time for more passing situations. Lack of width will allow the defence to concentrate in the most advantageous position.

Assessment:

Set up waves of attack emphasizing the need for width. Illustrate the effect on the defence and point out the increased passing possibilities.

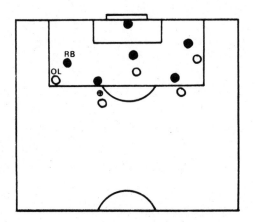

In the diagram the RB is controlling two players because the OL has come infield to an already congested area, making it easier for the defence to cover and possibly intercept.

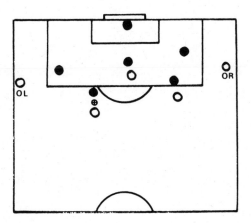

The attack has been mounted in good width and both wingers have room in which to manoeuvre. As a result, they will stretch the defence.

It is not necessarily the position of the ball carrier which creates width but the intelligent running of the other forwards.

Improvisation in Attack

Set up a small sided game (5 v 5) and stress individual skill and imaginative running by the men off the ball to create passing possibilities.

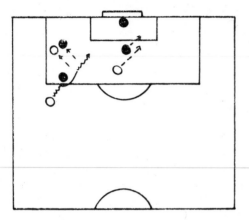

Show supporting forward how to draw off cover by running at and past the defender to let the ball carrier take on his opponent in a 1 v 1 situation.

DEFENSIVE PRINCIPLES

Depth in Defence

To combat offensive depth, the defence must limit their passing possibilities by giving cover from behind. When defenders stand square or in line there are innumerable passing opportunities. Attackers can easily penetrate the defence and perhaps score a goal.

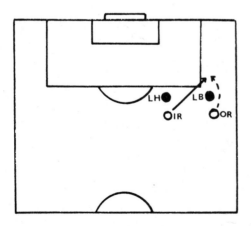

Here the LH and LB have been caught lying "square," and a through pass is open for the OR.

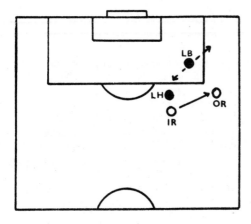

If the LB observes the principle of depth, he will drop back. In this position he can cover a pass to the OR or challenge the IR if he beats his man. In this way he can see both players and possibly anticipate his opponents by intelligent positioning.

Balance in Defence

Depth around the ball is not sufficient, however. It must be balanced as well. A defence can have good depth in an isolated area but still be in a vulnerable position because it is not balanced. To counteract offensive mobility, the defence must maintain control of attacking space at all times. They can do this by adjusting across the whole field and not just in the immediate vicinity of the ball.

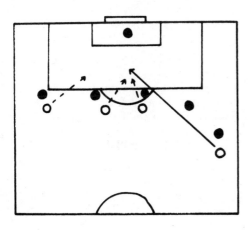

On the left side of the defence there is good depth, but not on the rest of the field. There is poor balance on the right side, as the players are standing in line with each other. Behind them is open space which the offense can run into and use to create passing and scoring opportunities.

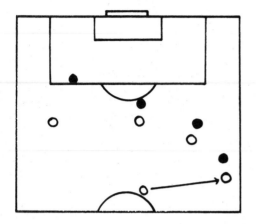

Balancing the Defence:

Set up four fullbacks plus four forwards.

Walk to positions (for balance) when the ball is played out to one side. The fullback moves forward to pressure the attacker while the left centre back moves across to cover behind him. The right centre back gives him cover and the right back balances the defence by lying deeper. Some coaches will prefer to play this fullback in line, with the centre back to restrict the forwards from more advanced positions. This tactic can lead to a flat rear line, increasing the chances of penetration on a through ball.

Delay in Defence

Delay is an essential principle of defence. On losing possession of the ball, initially the players nearest it should endeavour to delay the opposition long enough to allow their team to reorganize. This can be achieved either by quick man-for-man marking of players near the ball, tackling and chasing by forwards, which forces the opposition to use longer, more risky passes, or by backing off the player in possession and blocking the most decisive passing angle.

Assessment:

Observe how well forwards, in particular, tackle or harass opponents after being dispossessed or beaten to the ball. Illustrate the purpose of delay and show how they can effect it in the game situation.

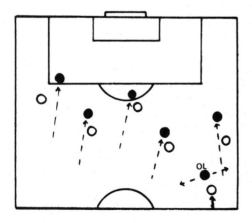

In attack, OL has lost possession to the opposing fullback. He has chased the man back, limiting his passing opportunities and delaying him so that his own defence has time to run back and take up position again.

DELAY = TIME = DEPTH AND SUPPORT

Concentration in Defence

If the defence plays a tight man-for-man system, it will be stretched by the width of the attack and will leave huge gaps for penetrating passes. They should funnel into the goal mouth and concentrate their defence there. The idea is to limit the passing and scoring opportunities and increase the possibilities of interception.

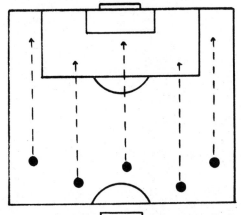

Running straight back—producing width in defence and leaving space for attackers.

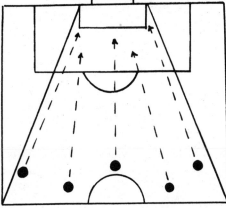

Funneling back towards goal to close space around danger area by concentration of defensive players.

Control and Restraint in Defence

In all interception and tackling situations, players must be confident, courageous and determined if they are to regain possession. Defenders must exercise control and restraint particularly when the opposition has the ball under control.

If the defence commits itself wildly or too early, it may jeopardize the use of other principles of defence and leave itself open to a penetrative attack.

Assessment:

Watch out for the tendency to lunge into a tackle without regard for the tactical situation or position on the field. Illustrate the benefit of exercising control and restraint until the defence is organized and an opportunity to intercept or tackle safely presents itself.

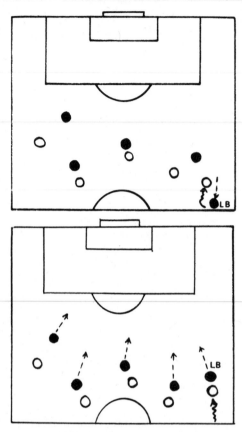

LB has tackled wildly in a bad position, leaving attackers with 2 v 1 options.

LB shows restraint by falling back as opponent advances in order to give his teammates time to get into defensive position.

By teaching how to respond to general situations, the coach is in effect teaching players the tactics of a system which can be applied to isolated situations. Also, by observing players as they work on a principle, the discerning coach can select players who assume certain responsibilities naturally or are able to carry out specific tasks. In this way players are picked for certain roles. The coach can build a pattern based on their ability to perform specific functions within the team. Reinforced through functional training, a flexible pattern of play is allowed to emerge. Rather than lay down a set system, outline what certain players are expected to do within that framework.

Strictly speaking, systems are merely the labels and the numbers attached to various formations. The real value lies not in the organization but in the understanding of the principles involved.

Only by practicing these situations will players begin to recognize them in the game and accept the functional responsibility of their roles within the pattern of play.

Limiting younger players to restricted positions is as bad as attempting difficult formations and asking too much of them. The happy medium, of course, is allowing some freedom within the bounds of their duties. Normally, the younger the age level, the less need for complicated defensive formations and negative play. Aggressive, imaginative play should be encouraged, and all players should have the chance to play their part in attacking the goal.

8
COACHING PRINCIPLES OF PLAY

Putting principles into practice is a problem for all coaches, but recognizing which principles are critically affecting the game is a bigger one. If, however, the coach teaches in terms of opposites, he can contrast principles of attack and defence, which will help players understand the game better.

The grid or box system of confined areas can be used again by marking off areas on the field and setting up realistic practices such as 3 v 1, 4 v 2, 2 v 1, 1 v 1, 3 v 3, 3 v 4, and 5 v 5. The coach can restrict space to control the practice.

As with the passing practices, the coach can run the drills emphasizing a variety of principles, or he can teach a principle by selecting drills which illustrate it. A discerning coach will decide which point, out of all the ones he might teach, he wants to emphasize the most in each practice. On that basis, coaching each principle in turn, I would suggest the following procedure:

Assessment. Play 5 v 5 in half field (forwards v defence) and illustrate the principle which you have decided to coach, or select principles which need attention.

Main Theme. Set up realistic situations (3 v 1, 4 v 2, etc.) in a confined area which feature the principle. Build up the situation by expanding area and introducing players (3 v 3, 3 v 4, etc.), still stressing the principle.

Game Situation. Practice principle in game situation (or original practice of forwards v defence) to work on principle in realistic context.

With this procedure in mind, look at the principles and the players. When possible, try to set up realistic situations where two principles (offense and defence) are in opposition. Pose problems to the players and, offering some guidance, observe how they solve them. In this way we may look at:

1. Offensive depth and defensive depth
2. Offensive mobility and defensive balance
3. Offensive penetration and defensive delay
4. Offensive width and defensive concentration
5. Offensive improvization and defensive restraint

DEFENSIVE DEPTH AND OFFENSIVE DEPTH

Assessment

Play waves of attack or five a side with no specific formation on either side. Simply stress support for the man with the ball in attack and zoning around the ball in defence.

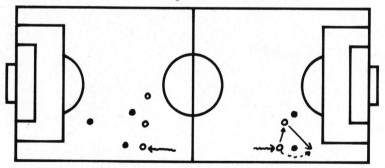

Good depth by defenders. Attackers show lack of imagination in their position.

Defenders too flat, open for through ball. Useful wall pass shown by attackers.

Main Theme: Depth in Attack

3 v 2

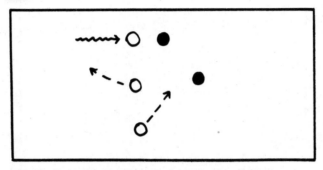

Intelligent running off the ball to give depth (therefore, support from behind).

3 v 3

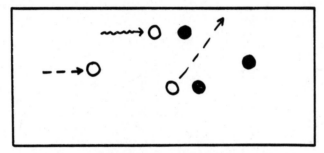

Good depth from safety man in attack—backing up forwards.

3 v 4

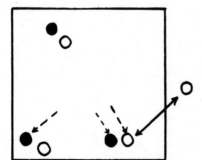

Players support man with the ball from the front. Three men are confined to box. They have to lose cover to support ball carrier and return pass one at a time, not bringing defenders to the ball.

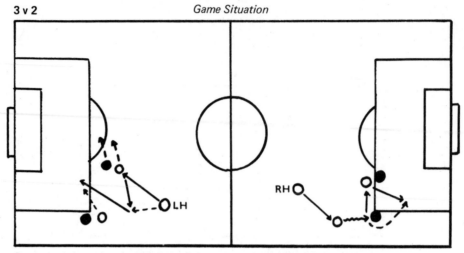

3 v 2

Game Situation

Set up and through pass. Depth from LH.   Wall pass depth from RH.

Main Theme: Depth in Defence

Set up situations where two or more defenders have constantly to adjust their positions in order to give support and prevent through passes.

3 v 2

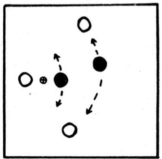

Front player pressures the ball carrier, limiting the passing angle, while rear player sweeps behind him to give cover support. If he goes to any of the free men, he will be caught in line with the other defender and will let by a penetrating pass.

3 v 3

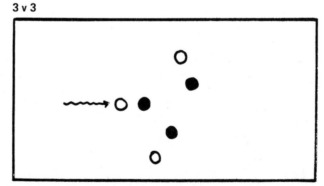

Good depth in attack is combatted by the depth of the defenders, who give cover support to the man pressuring the ball carrier.

Game Situation

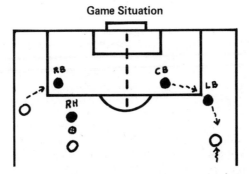

RB is in a position to watch the ball carrier and his opponent. By swinging behind the RH, he can give cover support.

If LB moves forward to delay attack, CB moves across to cover and give depth.

Application to Systems

Chapman of Arsenal is given the credit for developing the WM system. Withdrawing a central defender between the fullbacks closes attacking space in front of goal and between defenders.

In attack, the WM shape naturally results in numerous triangular formations which make it easier for players to support each other and maintain depth.

Rigid adoption of this system results in man-for-man marking, the fullbacks covering the wingers and the half backs covering the inside forwards.

If the coach uses this formation, he should practice methods of attack and defence against a team using the same system.

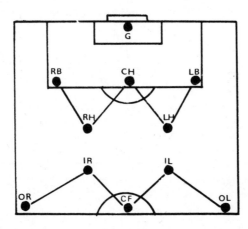

OFFENSIVE MOBILITY AND DEFENSIVE BALANCE

Keeping set positions imposes man-for-man marking on players. Under these circumstances, attackers should use mobility to penetrate while defenders should balance to maintain good depth.

Main Theme: Mobility

Use passing practices with no targets other than keeping possession initially. Players need to learn how to interchange positions rapidly.

3 v 1

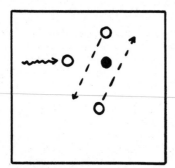

Open/blind side running to create space and time.

3 v 3

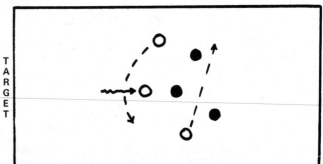

When targets are set up (end line of grid), encourage players to play both in attack and defence. There is no set role they have to play, other than running intelligently to receive the ball. One useful condition that the coach can impose: they may only play the ball forward. Therefore, they must be mobile to penetrate.

Game Situation

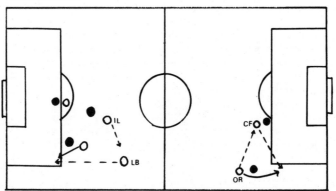

Overlapping fullback, LB assumes defence duties.

CF and OR exchange roles.

Main Theme: Balance

Show defenders how to react to a quick change of position by attackers; how to rebalance when the ball changes possession and is played past one of them.

3 v 2

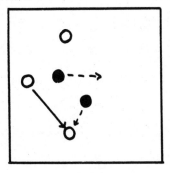

When ball is played past one defender the other moves forward and they reverse positions.

Game Situation

If the defence has been using the conventional WM formation, the three-man back line will pivot or turn around the centre back to give diagonal cover.

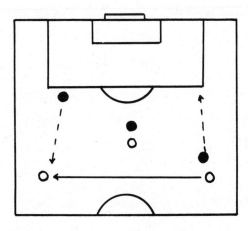

This practice shows the movements required to rebalance defence in the event of a quick switch of play across the field.

If the coach decides to use four rear defenders because of the threat of more mobile forwards, then he should try the following practices with his defence.

Switch of Play

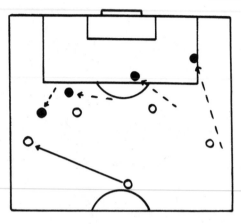

Pivoting the rear defenders.

Strike in Centre

One centre back moves forward to challenge the attack, while the other covers the space behind him.

By contrasting balance and mobility in this way the coach can develop the understanding necessary between players to read the game intelligently and react.

In attack, encourage intelligent, imaginative running, and look for players who are prepared to run constantly. In defence, look for intelligent anticipation by players and their awareness in covering mobile forwards.

Application to Systems

The interrelation of these two principles of play directly affects the formation of players and their duties.

1.

The effectiveness of mobility in attack was demonstrated to a great extent by Hungary in the 1950's. By withdrawing the centre forward they attempted to lure the centre half out of the middle, and the inside forwards became the strikers in the spaces between the fullbacks.

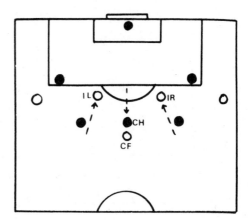

2.

This defensive problem was combatted by pulling a halfback into the rear line to play a four back system. This allows the two centre backs to cover the middle area and, if one is drawn forward, the other covers at the rear. In this way the defence attempts to close the decisive space between individual defenders in the rear line while conceding the space in front.

This development, coupled with a four-man forward line, whose advantages were just being recognized, led to the 4, 2, 4 formation.

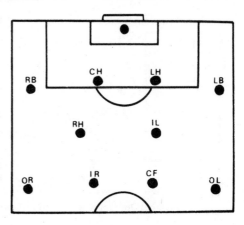

OFFENSIVE PENETRATION AND DEFENSIVE DELAY

The eventual aim of attack is to penetrate a defence and score. Penetration in soccer is usually attempted at speed in order to catch players off guard.

Main Theme: Penetration

Teach players to look for the through ball or penetrating pass. This is possible in situations where opponents are caught off balance and in line, either side by side or one behind the other.

3 v 2

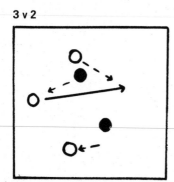

Through ball rather than safe square pass.

2 v 2

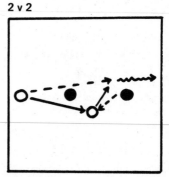

Play ball early, as close to defender as possible, to prevent wide run by supporting player.

Game Situation

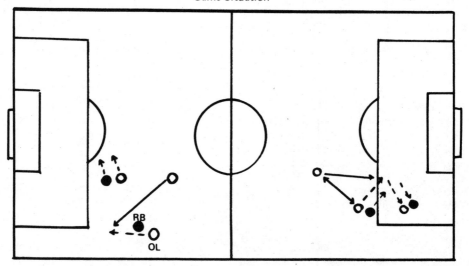

Through ball to winger inside RB.   Set up and through ball with exchange of position.

Main Theme: Delay

Set up a situation in which a player has to delay his opponent by narrowing his passing angles, show restraint in intercepting and give his teammates time to cover the opposition.

3 v 3

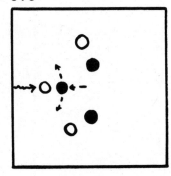

Coach pressure by nearest defender and cover support by teammates.

3 v 3

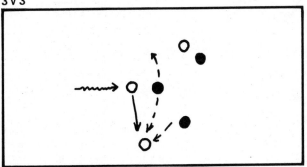

When the ball changes possession, a delegated player sweeps across mid-field or mid-area attempting to intercept or delay attack.

2 v 2 *With Returning Support*

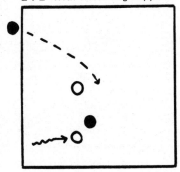

Attempting to delay attacker by intelligent positioning gives support time to return from deep position.

Game Situation

Winger runs back to delay attack by fullback.

Midfield link man becomes sweeper in front of defence.

Application to Systems

These principles can be incorporated into any system a coach might select. It is simply a matter of convincing players of the importance of these principles and helping them recognize when to employ them in the game.

Some coaches rely on a particular system to assist the team in using various principles.

A variation of the 4, 2, 4 system is this: withdraw a forward from the front line and use him as a centre midfield player to create a 4, 3, 3 formation. In this position, the player will further close the midfield space, which is exposed in the 4, 2, 4 system, and help lessen the intense demands of the two link men to delay attackers.

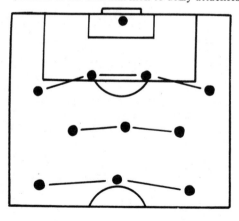

The three forwards have to use all of their attacking principles to succeed in penetrating. The use of an arrowhead formation overloads the two centre backs. The wing halves can also be released to overlap in attack because of the cover given by the centre midfield player.

OFFENSIVE WIDTH AND DEFENSIVE CONCENTRATION

Main Theme: Width

Illustrate the need for offensive width by setting up a tight situation. Players will immediately recognize success and failure:

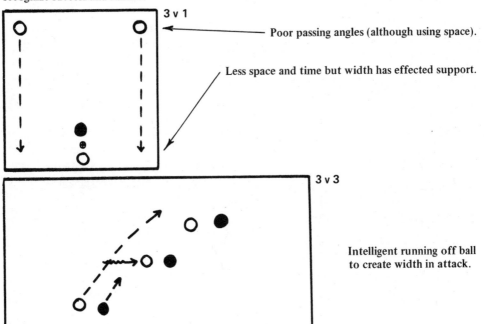

3 v 1

Poor passing angles (although using space).

Less space and time but width has effected support.

3 v 3

Intelligent running off ball to create width in attack.

Game Situation

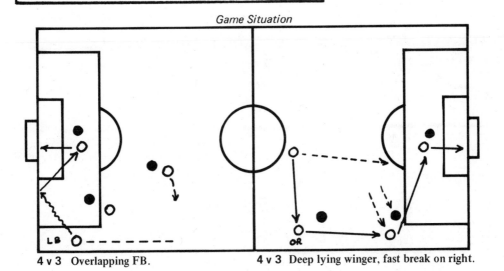

4 v 3 Overlapping FB.

4 v 3 Deep lying winger, fast break on right.

Main Theme: Concentration

Set up situations with targets to give players the feeling of funnelling to close space.

2 v 2

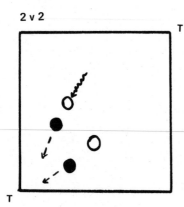

With target (T) in the corner, the shape of the defending area makes funnelling necessary.

Game Situation

3 v 2

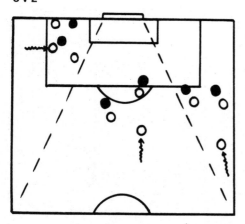

Divide the field into the areas defenders might normally play and set up situations with a ball in each area.

Application to Systems

Traditionally, the winger stayed out on his wing as wide as possible ready to start an attack. Today many systems of play use this wing or flank area in a similar way, but, stressing mobility in attack, it is not uncommon to find a fullback or halfback going down the wing on what is commonly referred to as an overlap run.

Most systems which use four rear defenders will use this tactic. The fullback knows that one of the centre backs will cover him from behind if he decides to go on an overlap. The danger of penetration from this area forces the opposition to concentrate in the vulnerable area around the penalty box. There are a variety of methods for concentrating and for reducing the space between and behind defenders.

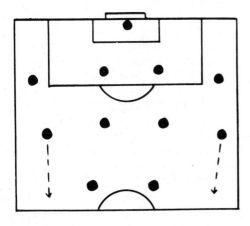

The 4, 3, 3 system concentrates defenders by playing them in rows. Another variation, the 4, 4, 2 system, results from pulling the wingers of the 4, 2, 4 back into the midfield line when possession is lost.

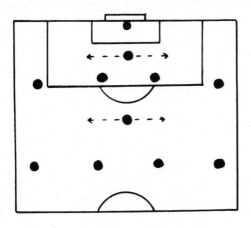

The sweeper used in systems of play is usually a free man who moves in from behind the rear defenders to "sweep" up any penetration of the defence.

There are several variations of the sweeper formation. One of the centre backs can take this responsibility, for example, and in some cases the goalkeeper may opt to play a more active role in intercepting any through balls that enter his penalty area.

OFFENSIVE IMPROVISATION AND DEFENSIVE RESTRAINT

The ability to do the unusual or the unexpected is becoming more and more necessary to successful attacking play, due to the better organization of defence.

Success normally depends on individual skill, but using the principles and relying on the awareness of other players is also important.

Main Theme: Improvisation

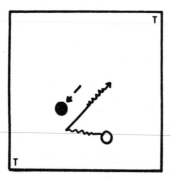

2 v 2   **Target**

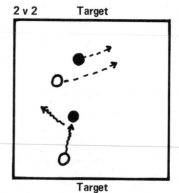

Target

Deliberately encourage dribbling skill in a 1 v 1 situation with two targets (T).

Coach—Committing the defender by running hard. Committing the defender to one direction. Changing pace/direction/faking to reach target.

Practice dribbling for penetration (mobility by free forward destroying cover).

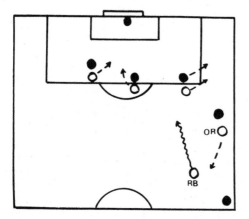

Game Situation

RB, having intercepted a pass to the winger, is able to carry ball deep attack because of cover given by his own OR and the space-making runs of the other forwards.

In small-sided coached game show players HOW, WHEN AND WHERE to run in certain situations to open up other possibilities. A dribbling condition of having to beat a man before passing will stress individual skill.

Main Theme: Restraint

Set up situations where defenders have to time the tackle by "jockeying." This involves feinting while running backwards.

1 v 1

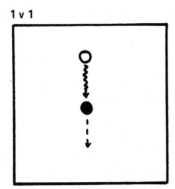

2 v 1

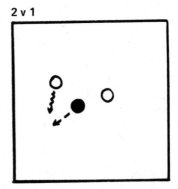

In this man-to-man situation, the defender backs off and shows restraint until there is an opportunity to dispossess his opponent.

The defender feints the tackle while attempting to cover pass to supporting player.

Game Situation

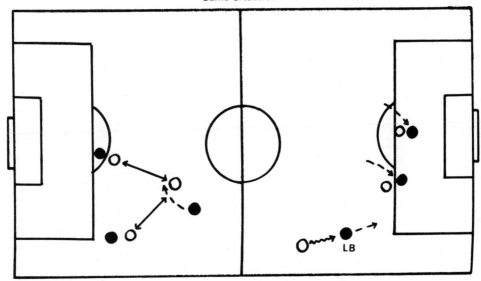

Defence shows restraint in setting up play, refusing to be drawn into tackle. This gives time for forward to tackle back and help.

Retreating FB gives defence time to organize.

9
CONDITIONING METHODS

A review of the literature on soccer conditioning methods shows many different schools of thought and a variety of methods for achieving fitness.

The purpose of this training programme is to familiarize the North American coach with the current methods of conditioning and indicate what the benefits are in terms of fitness. Generally, the individual coach has his own ideas on fitness and tends to select the methods which he is familiar with.

I would caution, however, that many training methods are based either on tradition, individual ideas or the training methods of other sports. Due to the lack of comparative experimental research in soccer, these methods can only be evaluated by means of already substantiated research in the field of exercise physiology. By consensus, the physiological components of fitness important to soccer are:

1. Endurance/Stamina
2. Speed
3. Strength and Power
4. Agility/Mobility

Conditioning for the Goalkeeper

The goalkeeper requires special conditioning. Physiology studies have shown that the goalkeeper does not need as much general endurance training as other players but that, in specific endurance, he has more demands made on him during a game and needs conditioning in this area.

There is little point in subjecting goalkeepers to the amount of running which the rest of the players undergo. They don't need running speed but agility and reaction speed. To this end, they should be specifically trained to endure pressure. Perhaps more than any other player, the goalkeeper should constantly be involved in live situations where he is under pressure. He should, of course, take part in warm-up activities as outlined, with special emphasis on the agility work. Circuit training and weight training are particularly applicable because of the short explosive bursts of violent muscular activity characteristic of the position.

Conditioning practices with the ball in competitive situations can be adapted for the goalkeeper by allowing him to intercept with his hands or dive on the ball.

ENDURANCE AND SPEED

Soccer demands stamina. Players have to keep going for ninety minutes, and frequently sprint, both with and without the ball. Physiologists call the ability to keep going at a moderate pace aerobic (with oxygen) exercise. The player replaces any oxygen used up as he is working on a pay-as-you-go basis. For example, a fullback falling back easily into defence when the opposition gets possession of the ball doesn't get winded.

The other kind of exercise is called anaerobic (without oxygen), meaning that a player often has to work for periods when he cannot pay back the oxygen he is using up until he has finished working. For example, the fullback going on an attacking run receives the ball, reaches his opponents' penalty area, but loses possession and has to sprint back into defence, arriving in position out of breath.

What does all this mean to the soccer coach? Simply that these two important factors must be incorporated into his training methods. First of all, the general endurance needed to keep going for ninety minutes and, second, the specific endurance required for short periods of maximum effort during the game.

Preseason training should concentrate on general endurance in order to prepare the players for the more intensive demands of specific endurance. During the season, however, the major emphasis of training will be on specific endurance. This is not to say that general endurance should be neglected, but training studies have shown that the running involved in normal skill and scrimmage practices is sufficient to maintain fitness.

General Endurance—Preseason Training

Traditionally, soccer training consisted of continuous running or lapping of the field. This was done in the belief that the demanded this type of long distance endurance. Coaches eventually discarded it as inefficient. Even the marathon runners turned to other methods of training. With the advent of fartlek and interval training in athletics, these methods were adopted by soccer coaches.

Fartlek

Fartlek is a form of training featuring informal fast-slow running, as opposed to the formal fast-slow running of interval training. The pace should alternate between fast and slow, with a basic emphasis on fast running (preferably, although not necessarily, over natural surfaces such as golf courses and fields or through woods). This psychologically stimulating form of training, when properly executed, should develop both general and specific endurance.

The following is an example of the variety of activity which might be included in a two mile fartlek:

1. Jog ten minutes as a warm-up
2. Five minutes brisk calisthenics
3. Half mile at fast, steady pace—3/4 speed
4. Jog 1/4 mile
5. Three to four acceleration sprints of 150 yards (jog 50 yards, stride 50 yards, spring 50 yards), walk 50 yards after each
6. Four to six sprints of 20–50 yards, jogging 50 yards between each one
7. Jog 1/4 mile as a warm-down

This programme should not be attempted immediately at the start of the season. Coaches should adapt this type of programme to players' fitness levels. Some will be capable of much more than others. Youth soccer teams may concentrate practice over shorter distances, as in interval training.

Slow Interval Training

Slow interval training develops general endurance. Players run at a faster speed than in continuous fast-running training and are conditioned for more intense running. The heart beats at the rate of approximately 180 beats/minute during the "effort" or fast phase. Slow interval training is usually restricted to distances less than 880 yards. It includes repeated sprints of 100, 220, 440 and 880 yards.

The soccer field, which has a length of 100 yards, is perfect for 100 yard sprints. Line up players at one end line and time their runs to the opposite end. It is more beneficial for recovery to have them walk back to the starting point for the next sprint. The coach can blow his whistle at specific time intervals for players to gauge their sprint and recovery times.

During this initial phase, speed should gradually increase and recovery time decrease in preparation for more demanding training. For example, one month of slow interval training would involve:

Week 1
Pre-test each player to ascertain his best time on a 100 yard sprint with a running start. Add four or more seconds to the player's best time. As an example, if the player's best 100 yard time is 12 seconds, his time for repetitions of the 100 yard sprint in slow interval training would be 12 + 4 = 16 seconds.

Train players to gauge the desired speed of repeats by the number of whistle blasts, e.g., when they should be ¼ way, ½ way, ¾ way and at the finish line. For a 16 second, 100 yard sprint, whistle at 4, 8, 12 and 16 seconds.

Build up their ability to run 5 to 15 repeats at this pace, allowing them to decide when they are able to do more.

Week 2
Impose more rigid time limits on recovery times. For example:
5 × 100 in 16 seconds with
   60 seconds recovery.   Walk
5 × 100 in 16 seconds with
   60 seconds recovery.   Walk 2
5 × 100 in 15 seconds with
   60 seconds recovery.

Week 3
5 × 100 in 15 seconds with
   55 seconds recovery.   Walk 2–4 minutes
5 × 100 in 14 seconds with
   55 seconds recovery.   Walk 2–4 minutes
5 × 100 in 13 seconds with
   50 seconds recovery.

Week 4
5 × 100 in 13 seconds with
   50 seconds recovery.   Walk 2–4 minutes
5 × 100 in 12 seconds with
   45 seconds recovery.   Walk 2–4 minutes
5 × 100 in 12 seconds with
   45 seconds recovery.

Similar programmes can be laid out for 220, 440 and 880 yard sprints. A running track is better suited for these, but for the purpose of soccer training the 100 yard interval is more easily organized and is more characteristic of the game.

Training With the Ball

Many coaches also utilize game situations and running with the ball for fitness conditioning as well as variety. There has, however, been great doubt that these activities compare with interval training in terms of measurable speed and endurance benefits.

But recently, the Swedish physiologist

Agnevik, who was investigating how to train with the ball, established that it produced the desired effects provided the activity was properly controlled. From his investigations came the following practices for developing general endurance.

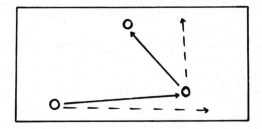

This is a typical techniques practice: passing, receiving and running with the ball inside a 20 × 10 yard area. It is also a good method for building stamina, because it makes demands on the aerobic processes. Players make quick passes, run after the ball and take up new positions, keeping this up for 3 to 5 minutes. After 3 minutes rest they go again for 3 to 5 repeats. But players must maintain a lively pace and be motivated.

Three or four a side soccer within a confined space (e.g., across the penalty box) for two minutes, rest for 1 minute and repeat 3 to 6 times.

Most players can, of course, continue these activities for much longer periods, but if they are to have the effects of interval training the coach must place these time limits on them. The introduction of coaching points can regulate the rest periods.

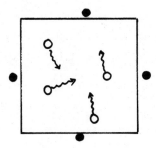

Two groups of four work alternately inside a confined area. One group works for 15 seconds, each player running and dribbling with a ball, while the other group rests. The groups change over and repeat 15 to 30 times.

Five a side soccer on a full field for 45 minutes. All players know how much stamina is demanded by five a side soccer on a full length field. This is recommended once a week, in order to increase the players' endurance capacity.

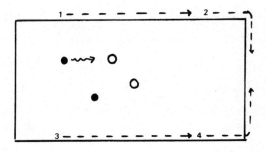

This practice is 2 v 2 inside an area 10 × 30 yards, with another group positioned outside the area. The object is to get the ball over the end line, but players 1, 2, 3 and 4 can assist the defending team. The groups change after 3 minutes work.

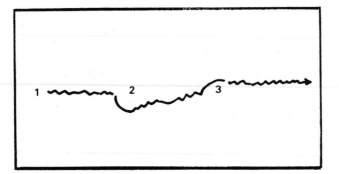

Dribbling practice across two grids. If A can dribble past B, he then takes on C. The object is to reach the far side of the grid. Repeat sequence for 2 to 3 minutes and change places. B takes the ball, then C.

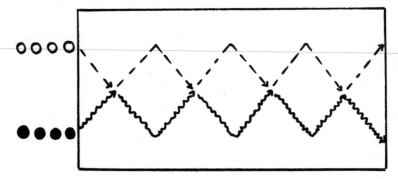

Diagonal running. Two players start about 40 yards apart, one with a ball and one without. Zigzagging, they exchange the ball when their paths cross, and continue this way down the length of the field.

Fast Interval Running

(Competitive Phase—Specific Endurance)

During the competitive phase of the season, the pace of interval running should become more intensive. In this method, players sprint all out for 30 to 40 seconds. This activity simulates the kind of stopping and starting found in the game and promotes specific endurance. In order to place stress on the anaerobic processes, the corresponding rest interval is reduced from an initial 90 seconds to 35 seconds.

These training principles can be used in various patterns to simulate game conditions and the inventive coach can devise his own practices to suit his particular facilities or age group. Here are some of the more common ones:

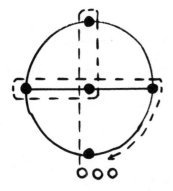

Clock or Triangular Running

Drop a number of markers around the centre circle about 5 to 20 yards apart. Specify the running pattern you want the player to follow, e.g., clock pattern of triangle run. If the coach uses colored markers or numbers, he can vocally instruct the player where to run. Players work for 30 seconds and rest while teammates work. Work with groups of 3 or 4 initially. These can later be reduced to 1 or 2 to decrease rest.

Maze Run

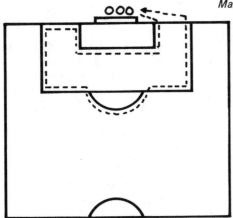

Here is a pattern utilizing the markings of the penalty area. Start players at 5 or 10 second intervals from a goalpost and have them follow the route outlined by the lines of the goal area and penalty box. Total distance covered will be 142 yards and should be run in 30 to 35 seconds. After 1 minute rest, players can be started again. For motivation, players can be started closer together and given the object of catching the man in front.

Sprinting around a 10 yard square, players reverse direction when they reach the starting point. They should run at full speed for 30 seconds, rest for 90 seconds, and repeat 3 to 6 times.

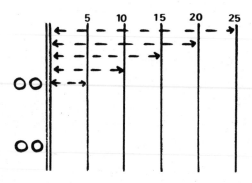

Set up relay races consisting of short sprints. Use 5 yard lines on a football field, or drop markers 5 yards apart. Each player sprints to the first line, returns to the double line, sprints to the second line and returns, etc. The total distance is 150 yards and should be covered in 30 to 35 seconds. The first man rests while the next player runs. Initially, with 3 or 4 players on each team, rest will last 60 to 90 seconds. By reducing the number on a team the rest interval can be decreased, depending on the condition of the players.

Obstacle Running

Lack of equipment need not handicap the inventive coach. For example, obstacle or maze running provides variety and competition if set up as a relay. It still provides excellent training if players work hard for 30 seconds.

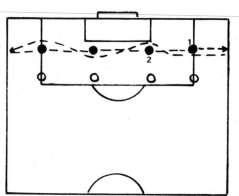

In 4-man relay teams, players can be used for obstacles. The first man in each team sprints to the side line, picks up a ball and sprints back, handing off to 2, who has moved up to the start. 1 continues to sprint, weaving between his teammates until he reaches the opposite sideline. On the return he has to leapfrog over and crawl under alternate teammates. When he reaches the starting point again, 2 starts his sprint, and 1 goes to the back of the team. Many variations of this are possible. With markers, flagposts and even hurdles, as in a school situation, much more can be attempted.

Conditioning With the Ball

Again, interval training with the ball is effective, provided the players work for 30 to 40 seconds at maximum effort.

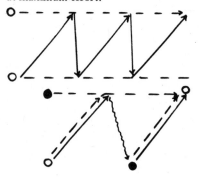

Two players spaced 15 yards apart run and pass a ball the length of the field. The ball should be played 10 to 15 yards in front in order to encourage quick bursts of speed.

This exercise is the same as above, only players receive, cross over and run with the ball before making the return pass.

With groups of two or three players the coach may want to incorporate some tactic or skill into this type of conditioning.

An extremely demanding practice with the ball is shown below: two players dribbling in a confined area. An efficient way of controlling the intensity of this practice is to use six players working in groups of two.

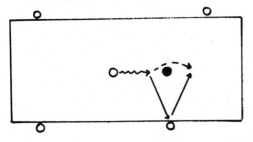

The object is to get the ball over the opposite end line and score a point. While one pair is busy in the centre, the other four players take up positions at each corner and assist in passing the ball. After one minute another pair takes over.

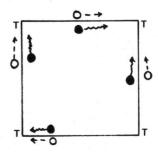

Dribbling Along a Line

Practice feinting and dribbling skills around the grid with the defender limited to his side of the line. Target (T) for ball carrier is one end of the line. Work for 1 minute, rest for 1 minute.

PRESSURE TRAINING

This has been a popular training method ever since its introduction by Winterbottom. It consists of submitting a player to a series of ball services that come in quick succession. He has to receive them using a variety of techniques. The coach, of course, controls the practice by controlling the service. Winterbottom used it to improve skill. However, if the service is designed to cause maximum exertion over a short period of time, the practice can be used for specific endurance conditioning rather than skill improvement.

The following circuit format is recommended. I have included some of the more common practices, but others can be substituted by the coach if he wants to stress particular aspects of the game. Players should strive for a high level of success with the technique involved and work as quickly as possible. As in other practices with the ball, motivation is the key.

Organization

1. Players should work in groups of 3 or 4 depending upon the degree of fitness. With 3 players, a player will work for 30 seconds and then rest for 2 × 30 while the other two take their turns.

2. Move around as a group to the next practice.

3. Always work in the same rotation for proper effect.

4. Players compete within their own group and with other groups for best score.

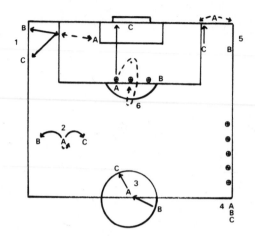

1. Sprint and Pass

   Player A sprints forward six yards to meet a ball passed from B. He passes it first time to C and runs back over the line to where he started, then sprints forward again to meet a pass from C. The number of passes he plays in 30 seconds is his score.

2. Heading

   Players B and C each have a ball and stand ten yards apart with player A in the centre. Player A has to turn, jump and head the ball back to each server alternately. The service should be quick enough for the ball to be in the air as A is turning.

3. First Time Passing

   Player A stands in the middle of the centre circle with B and C outside. B passes the ball to A and, at the same time, C calls for a first time pass, C then passing back to A while B calls for the ball. B and C can move around on the outside of the centre circle calling for the ball. The more time A takes to look for his man the less passes he will make in 30 seconds.

4. Shuttle Run

   Five soccer balls are placed in a line, each five yards apart with the first ball five yards from the starting line. On the word *go*, A sprints to the first ball and dribbles it back to the start, turns and collects the second ball, etc. The number of balls he brings behind the line represents the total score.

5. Receive and Pass

   B and C each have a ball and stand ten yards apart and five yards away from the goal line. A stands in between them but on the goal line. When the drill starts, A sprints to receive a ball lobbed by C into the corner arc, and passes it back. He then turns to sprint and receive a pass from B before it crosses the goal line, and passes it back— repeating for 30 seconds. Count the number of passes made as his score.

6. Shooting

   Player B places balls on the edge of the penalty box inside the arc. Player C returns balls from the goal. Player A has to run from outside the restraining arc and shoot a ball from the edge of the box, then run around the penalty spot and back outside the arc again before turning to shoot another ball. In this way the player runs 20 yards each shot. Count the number of shots taken to score each player.

Pressure Training for Goalkeepers

The principles behind the pressure training circuit also apply to the goalkeeper's training. He may work in a group of players but substitute his own specialties at each station, e.g., jumping to catch a ball instead of heading. The coach, however, may wish to train the goalkeeper separately and devise practices to strengthen him in places he is weak. Here are a few which are commonly used. The work-to-rest ratio is normally one minute pressure with one minute rest—3 to 6 repetitions for each drill.

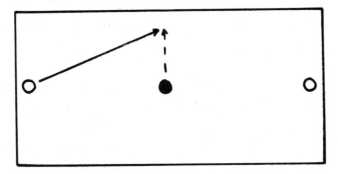

1. Goalkeeper stands in goal mouth or in between two grids. Players on each side of him each have a ball. Goalkeeper takes a throw from one player, making a save, then feeds it back to him. Immediately after, he turns to save a shot from the other player. The coach can instruct servers so that they stress fielding the ball at feet, waist or above the head, diving to save, etc.

2. Variation of this practice is to have goalkeeper keep his back to the thrower, who calls "turn" as he releases the ball, making the goalkeeper react quickly to the flight of the ball.

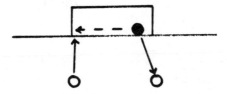

1. With goalkeeper in centre of real or makeshift goal, ball is rolled at each post by player one yard away. Keeper has to scramble from post to post to stop ball before it crosses the line. Number of contacts in one minute should be noted and compared to previous efforts to check motivation.

2. A variation of this practice is to move the opponents out to the six yard line and have them serve different kinds of balls towards the goalposts for the goalkeeper to collect and feed back again.

3. Further variety (and exhaustion) is possible by making the goalkeeper start in various positions, e.g., prone, before reacting to the ball. Or have him perform forward rolls between each save.

STRENGTH AND POWER

Although we stress certain exercises for certain components of fitness, a player should not be fit in one area and not the others. The coach has to consider fitness as a whole. Looking at the demands of the game in terms of speed and endurance, for example, he must recognize the importance of strength and power.

In current strengthening programmes for soccer, the most commonly used methods are Circuit Training and Weight Training.

Circuit training consists of carefully selected, simple exercises which are done around the perimeter of a field or gymnasium. The circuit is suited to large numbers. Players proceed from one exercise to another without causing undue local fatigue, but working up to individual capacity. Progress is achieved, initially, by decreasing the time of performance, and later, by increasing the load or the number of repetitions.

Circuit training is specifically recommended for the youth soccer coach who does not have the facilities for weight training, or who has an age group (under 12) which is too young for heavy strength training with weights.

The programme should be included in pre-season training to supplement endurance training but can be continued throughout the season. Initially it should be used at the end of training sessions to motivate players to make a maximum effort.

CIRCUIT TRAINING PROGRAMME

Done without any apparatus, circuit training makes use of the player's own body weight. Players can also train with light weights. The coach can vary the exercises and number of stations depending on what apparatus he has to work with and the number of players involved. But, in organizing his rotation, he must consider the effects each particular exercise will have in terms of strain. The good coach will avoid overloading any muscle group with strain by not running the same or similar exercises one right after the other.

The brunt of the exercises should, of course, fall on the legs, but consideration should also be given to abdominal and general body exercises. For example, a typical short circuit for soccer players might consist of:

1. Half Squat Jumps for Legs
   Player crouches until knees are at approximately an angle of 90°. (Do not encourage players to touch heels with hips as this can cause damage to knee joint.) From this position drive up off ground and extend legs in the air, landing in a crouch. Repeat.

2. Push Ups for Arms and Shoulder
   Lying prone with toes curled for traction and hands placed below shoulders, push up. Extend arms, keeping body straight, then bend arms and touch chest on floor. Repeat.

3. Trunk Extension
   Begin in prone position, hands clasped behind neck. Keeping legs still (partner can anchor), lift shoulders and chest off ground as far as possible. Lower, and repeat.

4. Squat Thrusts
   From standing position, drop to a crouch, with hands flat on floor, thrust feet backwards into a push up position, jump back to crouch and stand erect. Repeat continuously.

5. Sit Ups for Abdominals
   Player lies on back with knees bent, feet flat on ground and hands clasped behind his neck. Sit up until elbow touches opposite knee.

6. Shuttle Run
   Sprint between two markers spread ten yards apart, bending to touch the marker at each end as you turn.

Organization

There are various methods of conducting a circuit training session depending on the age level and motivation.

Individual Training

One of the distinguishing features of circuit training is, of course, the fact that the coach can have each individual player work at his own rate and own capacity rather than have all players do the same number of repetitions. If this individual training is adopted, it becomes necessary to pre-test each player's ability before establishing training loads. To pre-test, simply find how many repetitions of exercises 1, 3, 4 and 6 they can do in a minute. For exercises 2 and 5 they should do as many as they can, with no time limit. To calculate training loads, simply halve these results. This will be the number of repetitions of each exercise the player will complete on the circuit.

A training session typically consists of three circuits done as fast as possible. Re-testing should be carried out to establish new training loads and to see if the circuit is being used regularly.

In school, players normally enter their training loads on an individual card and check their number at each station. This is difficult to do in the field unless the coach keeps the players' records and reminds them of their loads.

The danger with poorly motivated groups, of course, is that players may do less than they should and simply go through the motions, since each player is working at a different rate and it is impossible to supervise all of them at the same time.

Pre-rated Stations

A simpler method of organizing training loads is to specify average repetitions for each exercise. This method is not as individually beneficial as tailoring exercises to meet the needs of each player but proves to be a more effective way to motivate players.

In this procedure, pre-test as before and, depending on the range of scores for each activity, establish two or three categories (A, B and C circuits or red, blue and green circuits) of training loads.

Post a card at each station with the categories and training loads. For example:

PUSH UPS

A—15

B—10

C—5

Based on their pre-test scores, assign players to the corresponding training circuits—A, B or C. In practice, have players complete the specified number of repetitions at each station but run three circuits as quickly as possible. Target times can be established so that, once a player reaches that target, he can move up to the next circuit.

Timed Stations

This is another method to cut out paper work. Work the players at each station for a specific time. Motivate them to work as quickly as possible. In a typical session the coach will work them for 30 seconds, then have them move on to the next station and work there for another 30 seconds.

The rationale is that stronger players will do more repetitions than weaker players in the same period of time, but players have to be motivated to do this. Care must be taken with younger or weaker players because, if the time is not properly limited, they may be achieving more than half as much as they did in the pre-tests, at maximum exertion.

Each coach has to decide which type of circuit works best with his players, depending on their age and motivation.

Weight Training Programme

Only recently have soccer coaches begun to use weight training programmes seriously. The traditional belief and fear was that this activity caused players to gain weight and, therefore, slowed them down. There is no physiological substantiation of this belief, however, and coaches are now recognizing the value of training with weights, but, as in other sports, opinions vary concerning how to use them.

After getting into good general shape, the soccer player should begin the preparation programme for strength training during the preseason phase. He may, for example, participate in circuit training for a few weeks before attempting to work with weights.

When he progresses to the set system of strength training he can continue with this into the competitive phase of the season. Weight training studies have shown the set system to be an effective way of training. This involves doing an exercise, then repeating it after a brief rest. The idea is to use a total amount of weight that would be impossible to lift without a rest. The set system develops the power necessary for endurance activities such as pressure training.

Most coaches would agree that, working against light resistance, a player doing many repetitions can only improve muscular endurance and will not affect the amount of muscular strength. Weight training or any other form of strength training must include a few contractions at maximum or near-maximum tension.

Strength training studies indicate that 3 to 9 repetitions a set are the optimum number of repetitions for building strength.

The training programme, therefore, requires the repetition, after a brief rest, of a few almost maximum contractions of the muscles involved in each exercise. The number of repetitions is kept low, usually about 3 to 5 for at least three sets.

Before embarking on a strength training programme, the beginner should familiarize himself with the exercises and work into the strength programme slowly. He should select a weight with which he can perform at least ten repetitions, to practice the exercise. When he is familiar with each exercise he can add weight until he is only able to perform five repetitions. He will then build up the repetitions with this weight until he reaches a point where he is working with a weight he cannot lift more than five times.

Now the athlete can progress to the set system, attempting three sets of 5 repetitions of each exercise.

The following program of exercises will provide specific strengthening of the muscle groups involved in soccer, together with general body conditioning.

Clean and Press

A good general exercise useful for warming up and strengthening. This exercise, done correctly, teaches the proper mechanics for all weight lifting activities.

1. First of all stand close to the bar, feet shoulder width apart and insteps under the bar. Squat down bending at the hip and knees with heels flat on floor and back straight. Arms should be straight, gripping bar just more than shoulder width apart.

2. Drive the legs straight, keeping the bar close to the body while flexing at the elbow to support bar at shoulder level (clean position).

3. From this position, extend the arms to the stretch position overhead.

4. Return to squat position by bringing bar down to chest, keeping it close to body down to waist level. Keeping arms straight, squat with bar and return to starting position.

Half Squats

Start as in circuit training—with the barbell behind the neck. Squat until knees are at a 90° angle and drive up to straighten knees, bend to 90° squat again, and repeat.

Stepping

With the barbell supported as for squats, and the flat of one foot on top of a standard gym bench, player steps up, stands erect, and steps back down again.

Dead Lift

Bend forward at the hips and grasp bar shoulder width apart. Raise the trunk to the erect position, pulling the bar with straight arms to the thigh rest position. Lower weight to floor. Repeat movement.

Heel Raise

Stand with toes and balls of feet supported on a piece of 2 X 4, with barbell resting across the shoulders. Raise the body up on the toes as high as possible. Slowly lower the heels to the floor again.

This programme should be followed three times a week, preferably on alternate days.

MOBILITY/AGILITY

The nature of the game makes the importance of this component of fitness evident. Many training methods (the obstacle race, for example) stress agility, but attention should be paid to maintaining or sharpening mobility/agility as part of the warm-up, which prepares the players for more strenuous activities.

Warm-Up

The warm-up is important before all physical exertion and cannot be overemphasized, but is frequently neglected in many sports. In a running game such as soccer, where great demands are made on the cardio-respiratory system and other muscle groups, it is imperative to prepare the body.

The most frequent acute injury in soccer is the torn muscle. Preventive treatment consists of eliminating the possible causes: poor circulation, inadequate training, or cold. Here an extremely important role is played by muscular warm-up, which every athlete must make a practice.

First of all, try some light running and jogging to raise body temperature. Do this before engaging in more strenuous running. The rule of thumb for the coach is normally to end this period when perspiration and flushing of the face appear, but most coaches don't push players hard enough in the warm-up. However, after the running, stretching and agility exercises can be performed with less danger of muscle strains.

A variety of running activities, minor games and exercises can be tried during this period. Here are some ideas which you can select from.

Preliminary Warm-Up

Jogging
1. Jog 50 yards; repeat three or four times.
2. Jog, kicking one leg forward/upwards and then alternately. Repeat three or four times.
3. Deep breathing in between each exercise.
4. Walking—arms circling.
5. Walking—trunk turning, arms carrying across body.
6. Jogging—touch right foot with right hand, then left foot with left hand and repeat three or four times—short walking sessions between each repeat.

After this preliminary loosening, the activities should now begin to be done at a quicker pace.

Running
1. touch ground on right side then on left side
2. go forward, turn sideways, both left and right
3. go forward, check to left and then to right
4. high jumps, arms reaching to sky
5. high jumps, heading imaginary ball
6. do knee raise and turn it outwards, singly, then alternately, with both
7. left leg kick across the body followed by right leg kick across body
8. run forward—turn—run backwards—turn—run forwards
9. run forward—turn and kick left and right as high as possible
10. at speed and on command, touch ground to left and then to right.

One Mile Continuous Warm-Up

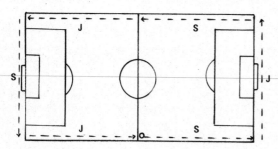

1. One lap of field in 3 minutes
2. One lap of field in 2–1/2 minutes
3. One lap of field in 2 minutes
4. One lap, alternating between 50 yard sprint and 50 yard jog

After this session, stretching and agility exercises can be performed with or without the ball.

EXERCISES WITH THE BALL

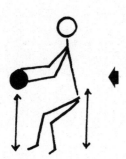

1. Bounce the ball with both hands and jump with the rise and fall of the ball.

2. Circle trunk with ball while holding it overhead with arms extended.

3. Limbo twister. Bend back and pick up ball lying on ground either directly behind or slightly to the side.

4. Hip circling. Circle the ball around the body while rhythmically circling the hips.

5. Move ball in a figure eight around the thighs, raising them alternately.

6. Bend slightly forward to a straddle position and move ball in a figure eight around the ankles.

7. Bounce the ball with both hands while kicking an extended leg over the ball.

8. Crouch. Bounce ball vigorously on ground and jump up to head the descending ball, go after the header and control it instantly.

9. Stand in straddle position, arms extended with ball overhead. Swing down and toss the ball in a high arc upwards between the straddled legs. Turn and control the ball instantly.

10. Sit with ball in hands. Toss ball in air, head descending ball, get up without use of hands and control the ball instantly.

11. Stand in straddle position with arms extended, holding the ball overhead. Drop the ball, turn, and try to control it using various techniques.

12. Stand with arms extended and raise the ball high. Kick up and touch the ball. Alternate feet.

13. Stand on right leg, knee bent. Raise left thigh, arms extended forward with the ball. Drop ball and flex lower leg to kick ball up to hands, catch, and repeat while keeping perfect balance. Alternate legs.

Warm-Up Games

As with the mobility exercises, these games are suited to a variety of purposes. In this chapter we are concerned with their use as a warm-up, but individually they make useful games for coaching skills.

Heading Games

This is a useful warm-up that also focuses attention on heading skill. The skill situation is difficult to simulate because of irregular services. To advance with the ball, throw, head and catch it. Head ball at small goal to score. If sequence breaks down, opponents restart game with throw. Variations:

1. Continuous heading—restart with head.
2. Basketball passing—set up to head at goal. Defence must intercept with head.

Passing Games

Possibly the best warm-up of all is the game itself in various forms. For example: indoor or five a side soccer, depending on the facilities. Played as an open running game with conditions (two touch or first time passing), they cause enough movement for adequate warm-up and provide good coaching vehicles.

Variations of this are to use spare men on the attacking side who change sides when the ball does—invaluable for young players learning principles of play, both offensively and defensively.

Rotation game. Number players from 1 to 5 or 7. The ball advances from 1 to 2 and so on. If intercepted by 3 of the opposition, he should continue the rotation to 4. The game demands intelligent running and positioning, and distributes the work load evenly.

Numbers game. This is best played indoors with two groups, each defending an end wall of a gymnasium. The coach calls numbers 2, 5 and 7, who play 3 v 3 to score past the defending "wall." Change numbers and size of teams. The game involves all players equally and provides coaching situations. To produce more understanding of principles of play and responsibilities, introduce more goals in the form of benches or side walls.

Four goals. Using four targets, have a pair of players defend each goal and attack any of the three other goals. If a pair scores, they leave and another two defend that goal. Again, this is useful for coaching principles and responsibilities.

Grid Games

The grid system, or any small area, lends itself to a variety of passing games from 3 v 1 in one area to 4 v 3 across two grids. Expanding the area and the number of players produces more involvement and coaching situations. I have outlined all of these situations in the section on passing. If these grid situations are carried out on a time and pressure training basis, they become extremely demanding and will result in more conditioning. The coach must be careful to produce the effect he is trying to achieve in a specific practice.

Dribbling Games

This is a kind of game to use after teaching dribbling skills. In a grid, or a small-sided game, players must keep possession of the ball (no passing allowed) and dribble it over an end line. A variation which produces more involvement is to stipulate that players must beat one man before they are allowed to pass. The coach can control the conditions to accentuate skills practice or running with the ball.

Tackling Games

Similarly, this game can be controlled to accentuate tackling or interception, but, if the players move the ball around it is difficult to focus on tackling. Therefore, after teaching tackling skills in smaller situations, integrate a dribbling condition into this practice in order to increase the opportunities to tackle.

10
RESTARTS

Soccer, being by nature a fluid game, rarely lends itself to the use of set plays. Restarts, however, are the exception. In these situations, possession is everything. If the attack gets the ball, it stands to gain increased penetration and possibly a goal. The defence is under constant threat and has to be ready for surprises. The advantage to the attack in corner kicks and free kicks is generally obvious. The other restarts have traditionally been regarded as necessary only to get the ball back into play, and often neither side pays much attention to the offensive and defensive principles involved.

For the defence in particular, set plays are considered crucial. No matter how unwilling a coach may be to use set plays in attack, he cannot overlook the fact that, in defence, his goal is threatened. Most coaches have definite views on offensive plays and on ways to combat them, and some believe in precise drilling for specific situations. Repeated practice of restart plays has much merit, but, rather than list all the set plays possible in restarts, let us consider the basic offensive and defensive principles concerned.

SPACE

The creation of space affords more time for the successful completion of skill. In all restarts, with the exception of the throw in, the opposition is restricted by at least ten yards because of the rules governing the restart. Therefore, the offensive team has an opportunity to use this space to its advantage. The defence will attempt to close this space as

soon as the ball is kicked in order to increase its chances of interception. In tight situations, the offensive team has to use increased skill, since there is little space. But more important than the space in front of the defenders is the space between and behind them, which the offense should try to take advantage of.

MOVEMENT

In order to create more space, intelligent movement by the offense is necessary; otherwise, it will be easily covered. If the defence persists in man-for-man marking, more space may be opened up by decoy runs. The tactic

of covering zones or areas of the field rather than individual players may prove more advantageous to the defence, in which case the conflict will develop into a contest of mobility versus balance.

SELECTION

The onus in offense falls on the player taking the restart. Depending on the space available and the possibilities created by intelligent mobility, he has to decide who is in the best position to receive the ball. If the defence has prepared for the restart and retains its balance, despite the attempts of the offense to throw them off, the selection should be limited and pose no immediate danger to them.

In addition to the principles enumerated above, the coach should analyze what principles of play are involved in each kind of restart, and use this knowledge in offense and defence to set up good plays for each situation. Let us look at some basic restarts in this way.

Kick Off

At the start of the game, or after a goal has been scored, the team kicking off has an immediate advantage—penetration—and can capitalize on it. The offense should try to exploit any initial lack of depth or balance shown by the defence as it lines up for the kick off. However, this involves more than simply kicking the ball as far up the field as possible, since there is no point in the ball penetrating without a player accompanying it! After the ball has been put into play, if the offense passes it back to one of its players, he is set up to select the most penetrating pass. This will depend on his attackers' movement: lining up with poor initial balance, or moving into vulnerable defensive area, or rushing towards the ball.

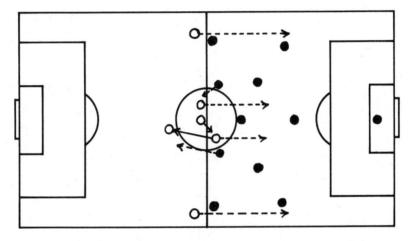

Fullbacks have been caught flat and close to centre line at the kick off. Opposing forwards have rushed to intercept the ball at the kick off, leaving space in midfield. If offensive players move quickly towards those spaces then the man on the ball has a number of good targets to choose from.

To stem this danger, the defence must maintain balance at all times. One player may be delegated the responsibility of rushing the ball in order to delay the penetrating pass while the remainder concern themselves with maintaining balance and adjusting to cover the penetrating runs of mobile forwards.

Throw In

When the ball is put out of play over the touch line, the game is restarted by a member of the other team throwing the ball back into play. This rule of the game was invented as a convenient way to restart the game and give the non-offending team possession of the ball. Many coaches, however, consider this a disadvantage as they have one man off the field (taking the throw) and the attackers can be closely covered to prevent possession being regained.

The coach should recognize that possession and penetration are the priorities of the throw in. In attack, players must remember the principles of mobility and improvization to create sufficient space to receive the ball. They have one advantage—they cannot be ruled offside at the throw in, and therefore can take up, or arrive at, advanced penetrating positions before the ball is served to them.

In defence, the defenders need to exercise great control and restraint to prevent being faked into poor positions and have to concentrate on maintaining balance in defence at all times. Let us look at some typical plays.

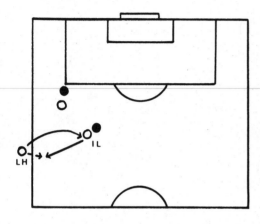

The forwards have created initial space by taking up position 5 to 10 yards from the thrower. In this way they have created space to move forward and receive the ball, as defenders will normally take up positions between the player and the goal. The LH throws to the IL, who is covered but passes the ball back first time to the LH. Possession is regained, and the LH is in a position to make another pass.

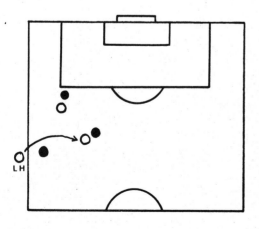

To counter the return pass, a defender could pick up the LH, after he has taken the throw, as there is no restriction of distance from the thrower at the throw in.

In this way the defence maintains its depth around the ball and has a man-on-man situation if the attack gets possession of the ball.

The more organized the defence, the more imaginative the attack has to be. Cover can be destroyed if players know when, where, and how to run.

There are many techniques for coaching players when to run. At the throw in, the receivers normally take up stationary positions and then react with a quick burst of speed or change of position at the thrower's signal (e.g., bouncing the ball, or slapping it with a hand). It is better for a player to arrive in a space late and move onto a ball at full speed rather than arrive too early and be covered by a defender in a static position.

Knowing where to run can be taught by having players run in pre-planned directions in practice, but generally players have to react to different situations. They must be able to read the situation if they are to know the best places to go (e.g., into an open space to receive the ball, or into a supporting position to allow someone else to receive it).

In the context of a throw in, the technique of running is important. Each player should be aware of the effectiveness of running *at* and *past* defenders to lure them into a decoy run, and of running on the "blind side" of defenders in order to arrive in position without being covered.

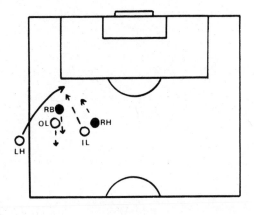

The OL and IL change positions hoping to draw a defender with them. The thrower has to time his throw so that the ball is collected on the run.

The OL draws the RB forward, creating space for the IL.

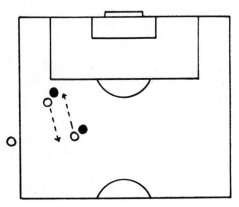

In this way each defender will pick up the man who comes into his zone and can intercept if the ball is thrown towards him.

If the defenders fall for this ploy, they can be instructed not to follow the player but to play in a zone defence.

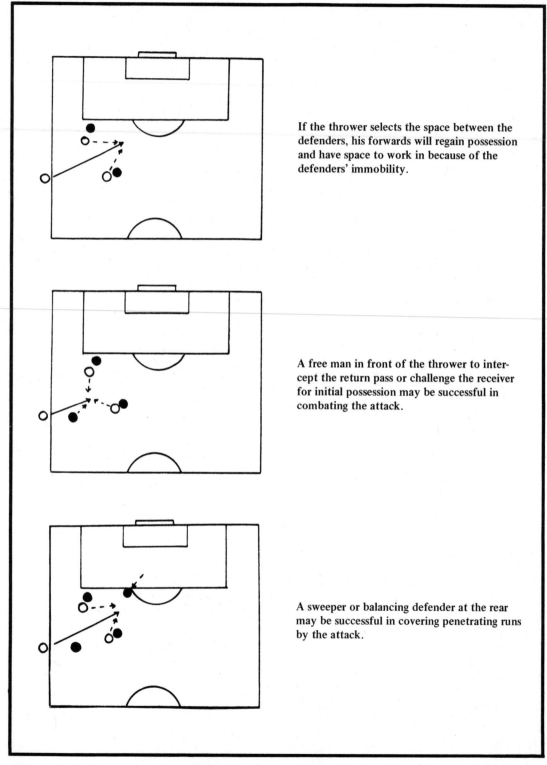

If the thrower selects the space between the defenders, his forwards will regain possession and have space to work in because of the defenders' immobility.

A free man in front of the thrower to intercept the return pass or challenge the receiver for initial possession may be successful in combating the attack.

A sweeper or balancing defender at the rear may be successful in covering penetrating runs by the attack.

Selection

We have already seen in the previous diagrams how the thrower's selection is influenced by the players' movement. When he has little choice, he will normally attempt to keep possession and build up an attack, but ideally he will throw to the man who has penetrated deepest, which will give possession behind the greatest number of defenders.

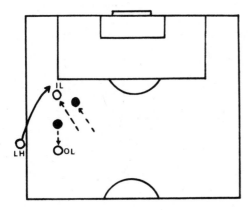

Given a choice of safe possession to the OL or penetrating throw to the IL, the thrower selects the most penetrating throw, i.e., to the IL.

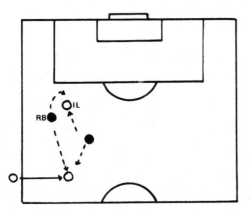

Against the threat of a penetrating throw, the defence may decide just to cover the most dangerous possibilities and sacrifice possession in less exposed areas of the field.

Rather than be drawn towards the ball, the RB is prepared to sacrifice possession in this instance in order to cover the penetrating IL, a more dangerous threat.

Goal Kick

By virtue of the fact that the goal kick is taken from the defenders' end of the field, it has not been regarded as an important restart from an attacking point of view. The most common kind of goal kick is one that sends the ball as far upfield as possible, in order to put the ball in the opponents' half of the field and increase the chances of penetration and attack. Unfortunately, when little thought is given to the tactics of the goal kick, the defence can normally clear the ball, since it is comparatively easier for defenders to head or kick the ball clear than it is for a forward to control the ball and turn with it. However, a long goal kick can be successful if it can be accurately directed to a target man upfield and supporting players take up the available space.

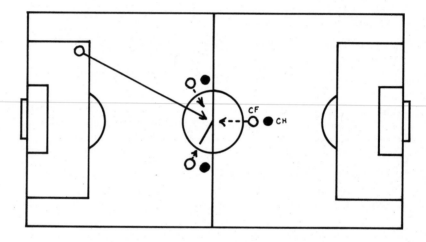

Here the CF has created space by pushing too far upfield. From this position he can move back towards the ball from the long goal kick and pass it off into the open space for his supporting forwards to collect. If the CH gets to the ball first and clears it poorly then supporting players can move onto it quickly.

The short goal kick can be used to allow the goalkeeper more choice in distributing the ball. By passing the ball out of the penalty area to a defender, who gives it back to him, the goalkeeper has the choice of punting, drop kicking or throwing the ball, depending on his preference or the range of his target. Often the goalkeeper is more accurate in throwing than in kicking, and many goalkeepers can throw as far as they can kick the ball.

The desirability of penetration by putting the ball as far upfield as possible, however, is tempered by the possibilities of possession. A comparatively recent trend in the use of goal kicks has been to play the ball out short but safe to a man in the clear. This, coupled with the changing role of the fullback, has in many instances meant the use of this player developing, or being involved in, an attack from deep positions.

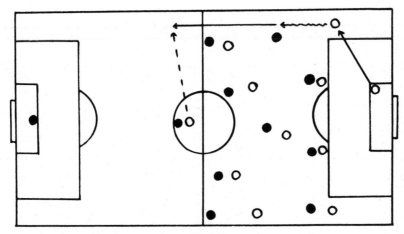

Fullback receives a short goal kick and starts an attack by carrying the ball or passing it up to a forward.

Defensive players should move aggressively against a long goal kick at the moment the threat first appears. They should meet any danger immediately, as it is comparatively easier for them to clear the ball than for the offense to control it. It is important for the defence to keep in balance and to commit a player to challenge a short goal kick. Control and restraint must be exercised in attempting to challenge, as this may be a way to obtain clear possession and start an attack.

Corner Kick

The corner kick has always been recognized as an important scoring opportunity. The ball can be kicked into the goalmouth from this restart. Often the outcome of the corner kick is a battle of the giants: a tall forward and tall centrehalf attempting to head the ball. There are, however, many variations possible.

Long Corner

If the kicker decides to play the ball directly into the goalmouth, he has a number of possibilities.

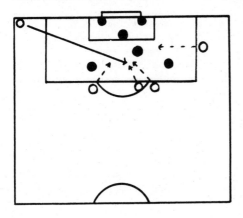

Here the ball is hit hard across the penalty spot. The forwards have withdrawn to the outside of the penalty box before starting their run. In this way they create space to move forward into. By running in with determination they will upset the defenders. If the first attacker misses the ball by jumping too early, he may leave a clear space for the next attacker to contact the ball.

COACHING POINTS

1. Don't start your forward run until you see the line of flight of the ball.
2. Time your run so you arrive in the right space "late" but going at full speed. This is better than arriving under the ball too early and having to jump vertically to contact it.

Defenders have to counteract any mobility of forwards by being mobile themselves. Otherwise, they are in a static position and at a disadvantage.

A variation of this long corner is playing the ball to unmarked player outside of the box, who can change the angle of the attack, and perhaps try a long shot.

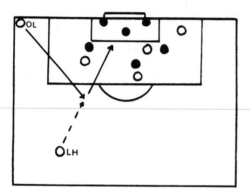

The OL drives ball deep to the LH, who in turn drives the ball back into the goalmouth.

An inswinging corner kick is often used with success to keep the goalkeeper in his area and to change the direction of the attack. The goalkeeper can be further troubled when awaiting the corner kick by a player positioned in front of him. This is not obstruction if the player moves away as the ball is kicked, and it often produces enough consternation to screen and unnerve the goalkeeper.

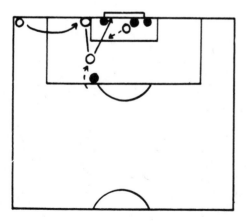

Here an inswinging corner kick has been played to a target man at the near post, who relays the ball back to a striker for a first time shot. The goalkeeper has been worried by a player in front of him and is unable to reach the ball early enough to cut the cross out.

Often a player in front of the goalkeeper will be able to score a goal himself from an inswinging corner by being in a position to reach the ball before the goalkeeper. From the initial set up, many variations can be worked out by changing the service.

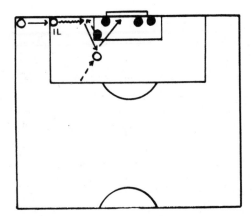

Short Corner

No defender has covered the IL, who receives a short corner and takes the ball as close to the goal as possible before being challenged, at which point he can either pass the ball off or shoot.

If a defender covers the IL, he has succeeded in utilizing the principle of width and has affected the concentration of the defence. But the defender can only come within 10 yards of the ball, so the IL can still safely receive the ball on the goal-line. Then he can try to beat the defender or cut it back to an attacker.

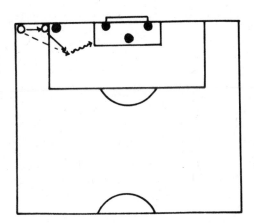

The OL passes to the IL and then moves to receive a return pass going in on goal.

If the attack succeeds in pulling two defenders out to combat the short corner, it has reduced the number of defenders in the area and may then take advantage of this additional space by playing a long corner.

Free Kick

The purpose of a direct or free kick is to get possession and penetrate. Following the basic principles, the attack will attempt to make space and the defence to cover any penetrating players and remain balanced. However, the closer to goal a free kick is awarded, the more advantageous and dangerous the situation is for the offense and defence respectively. The offense must decide at what distance it can launch a direct attack on goal, while consequently, the defence must be aware of the range at which they become vulnerable. Generally, most free kicks inside the attacking half of the field can be kicked into the penalty box. Therefore, defenders have to watch out for attackers taking up advanced positions to receive the ball.

Depending on the calibre of play, a direct shot from the average player will not be a threat unless he is within the 20 to 30 yard range. There is no need to attempt to block a shot outside this range, but it is often a good policy to put one player 10 yards from the ball to prevent the kicker from using a low hard drive to a forward. The other defenders would initially take up balanced positions, marking man-for-man. The closer they are to the free kick the tighter they mark the attacker, and the further they are from the ball the more they cover the space.

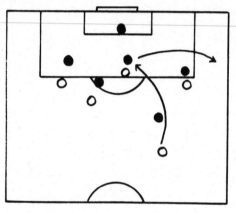

When the kick is taken about 35 to 40 yards from goal, the defenders have got to maintain depth. The goalkeeper has the responsibility of coming out about twelve yards from his goal to intercept any long pass into the area.

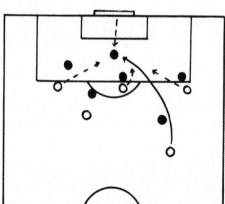

Long Pass

The defenders here are marking players close to the ball tightly, in an attempt to challenge a quick pass. Attacking plays from deep free kicks have to be extremely accurate or very well-timed to work.

A typical play is to attempt to drop a ball behind the defenders just outside the goalkeeper's range for a forward to run onto. This is a difficult spot to hit and most times is headed clear by a defender or picked up by the goalkeeper.

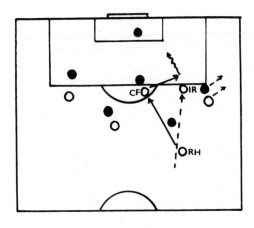

Dummy Run

Fakes or dummies in free kicks are often tried, but to be successful from deep positions they have to be extremely well-timed. For example, the IR fakes to take the kick but runs over the ball and keeps going, while the RH passes the ball to the CF, who relays it to the IR, who is able to take the ball in stride and go in on goal.

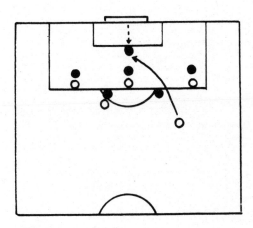

The closer the free kick is to the goal, the more the defence will employ tighter marking and take up flatter cover. This will prevent forwards from taking up advanced positions, while leaving the goalkeeper responsible for his 10 to 20 yard range outside the goal.

The use of a wall of defenders has become a common practice in blocking direct shots on goal. Each coach should formulate his own principles for the positioning and number of players and method of setting up the wall from various directions. The following guidelines should prove helpful.

There are various ways to set up the wall, but many are inefficient or against the rules of the game. The most successful way, in my opinion, is to line the players up about 6 to 8 yards from the ball in order to give a designated player (A) from behind the ball time to position a player (B) between the near post and the ball while the referee pushes the wall back another few yards.

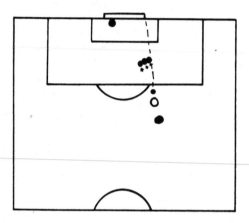

The goalkeeper moves to the far post to wait for the kick.

Positioning

The number of players in the wall is decided by the goalkeeper, who constantly watches the ball. The wall of players is usually lined up between the shortest distance from the ball to the goal, i.e., near post. The player at the near post end is lined up a half body width on each side of the post to prevent the kicker from shooting for the near post.

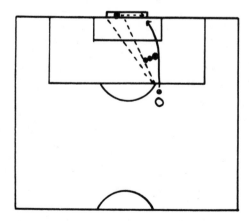

The goalkeeper normally positions himself just inside the far post so that he is defending only half of the goal against a direct shot. The "wall" is blocking the other half. If the ball is put over the top of the wall, then he has time to come across and intercept the ball. The theory behind this is that any ball shot over the shortest distance (near post) has to be lobbed, so he has more time to get to it. A direct shot over the longest distance (far post) he can watch longer and will have more time to react.

Number in the Wall

Opinions vary about the optimum number of players to have in the wall at various positions. Coaches may have their own ideas, but the goalkeeper should also be consulted. Here is a general guide:

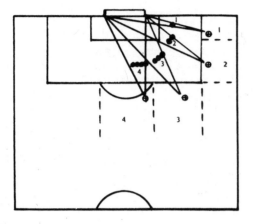

Four players for any free kick in front of goal in the area the width of the "D"—*never* split two players to each side.

Three players in the area from the edge of the "D" to the edge of the penalty box.

Two players in the area from the edge of the penalty box to opposite the six yard box.

One player in the area from the six yard box to the goal line.

The offense's opportunities for attack against a wall of defenders depend on the improvization of the attack and the efficiency of the defence. For example, the dummy run has to be extremely well-timed and accurate to be successful.

Here the IR has run over the ball and is just onside when the ball is passed through to him by the CF. He has timed his run to get away from the CH and to receive the ball from the RH.

Various other combinations for releasing a player behind the defence can be worked out by the coach. Other attacking plays are for disrupting the defensive wall or blocking the goalkeeper's sight.

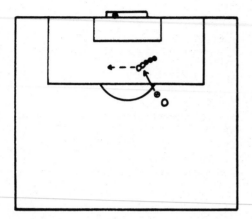

Here the attackers have formed their own wall beside the defensive wall in an attempt to block the goalkeeper's sight. The kicker has the option of chipping the ball over the defensive wall to the near post in the hope that the goalkeeper cannot see the flight of the ball until it appears over the defenders' heads. Another alternative is for the kicker to drive the ball at his own teammates, who break away at the last second. The idea is to surprise the goalkeeper, who may be anticipating a chip shot over the wall.

11
FUNCTIONAL TRAINING

Functional training of a player simply means focusing on some aspect of individual skill, or on his role in the game, which is done incorrectly. Ninety-nine percent of the time is spent on the individual·player or group having difficulty, although other players are introduced to make for a realistic game situation.

The basic principles to remember when conducting a functional practice are:

ORGANIZATION

1. Choose a realistic practice typical of the function or role of the player.
2. Always start practice with a service to the player in order to focus on his function.
3. Outline the target or aim of each function.

OBSERVATION

1. Observe the outcome of each attempt.
2. Decide if success is because the function is too easy.
3. Decide if failure is due to a lack of technique or a wrong decision made under pressure (challenge).

INSTRUCTION

1. If *technique* is poor, restrain the opposition to give the player more time to execute the movement properly.

2. If *decisions* are poor, give the player more alternatives for success in the form of supporting players or a safety measure.

3. If the player is reacting efficiently, then build up the practice to a completely live situation, perhaps a small-sided game, but still stressing the function of the player particulary concerned.

In this way, functional training will incorporate the advantages of a skill practice as opposed to pure technique training. Care must be taken not to increase the pace of the practice to such an extent that it becomes pressure training, or merely conditioning, in which there is likely to be a skill breakdown.

With this premise in mind, we can invent and introduce functions to various team members corresponding to their roles in the game. Here are some typical examples; many more can be introduced on the same basis.

Fullback

Involve the fullback in a typical situation and observe how he reacts.

Set up the function for a fullback (RB) of running back to control a through ball under pressure, then turning to find his target (the coach) with a long ball. From this simple situation we may build up by giving him other alternatives, and, in turn, cover them to influence his decision in selecting the correct answer.

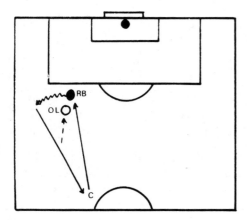

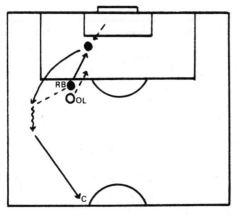

Instead of turning with the ball, he may choose to play it back to his keeper to take the return throw on the run as an attacking fullback.

In the figure above, for example, we have incorporated a former function of the goalkeeper and linked the functions together into *team play*. In turn, of course, we would cover the goalkeeper with another opponent, and then he may have to look to supporting wingers or link men, which will affect their own functions in the situation.

Here are some situations the fullback may find himself in:

1. Ball control after chasing an overhead kick.
2. Interception of a cross field pass to the wingman.
3. Balancing the defence, moving up to wingman, moving back to provide cover against a through ball past the centre half.
4. Dealing with high cross near goal.
5. Defending on the goal line when the goalkeeper is out of goal.
6. Dealing with a 2 v 1 situation.
7. Volley clearances upfield; volley pass to one's own wing.
8. Attacking play with wingmen and halfbacks.
9. Attacking at corner kicks, and defending against them.
10. Throw ins; taking the throw; defending against them.
11. Low drives to forward.
12. Placing free kicks.
13. Recovering and tackling again.

Centre Half

Consider the case of the centre back who is slow to make the correct skill response when under pressure. Set him up in a situation where he can utilize techniques with support, to improve his distribution of the ball.

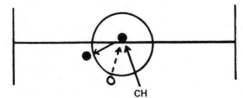

Restrain the opposing outside forward outside of the centre circle to give the CH enough time to make the correct skill response (passing to one of his supporting players). As skill improves, move the opposition closer to increase the pressure.

The following situations are also worthy of attention:

1. Heading from the goalkeeper's clearances.
2. Heading interceptions after corner kicks and high centres from the wingers.
3. Ball control to deal with the high ball, followed by a clearance kick or pass.
4. Passing situations—to the goalkeeper, to fullback, to the halfback.
5. Recovering after breakthrough by any forward.
6. Judging offsides.
7. Interception of both setting up and through passes.
8. Chasing, followed by tackles.
9. Clearance kicks—volley in a desperate situation.
10. Accurate use of long, low drives to the centre forward and wingmen.

His familiarity with the situation and his awareness of the supporting players' functions will help the CH's general team play.

Link Man

The link man, or halfback, is frequently called upon to switch roles, to change from supporting his forwards in attack to marking opposing forwards in defence. If we create a situation which brings out this changeover function, he should learn to appreciate better his responsibility as a member of the *team*.

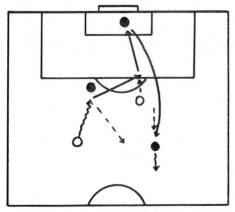

Play 2 against 3 attacking the goal. The link man starts with the ball, supporting his teammate in attack. If his pass is intercepted or a shot is saved by the goalkeeper, it will be quickly delivered to the opposing forward. The link man then has to think in defensive terms and chase back to challenge him before he gets over the halfway line.

The practice could be developed further by adding a covering link man, and an understanding of offensive and defensive roles could be coached.

Other possibilities for functions of this role include:

1. Playing behind an inside forward and wingman, including setting up and through passes.
2. Positioning and breaking through for a shot at goal.
3. Dealing with 2 v 1 situations; cover against wall passes.
4. Throw ins and corner kicks, both in attack and defence.
5. Linking with the other halfback in the first stages of an attack.
6. Quick service for the forwards, crossfield passing.
7. Defensive heading near goal.
8. Ball control in tight situations.
9. Short push passing—wall passing with a fullback, inside forward or wingman.

Wing Play

The function of wing play has become the consideration of all forwards, and often attacking defenders who "overlap" in this area of the field. Therefore, the following functions of wing play must be dealt with:

1. Committing the defender—techniques of dribbling.
2. Choice of moving to inside or outside of defender, i.e., right or left.
3. Defensive duties if possession is lost—chasing to delay or tackle.
4. Destroying cover by intelligent running when not on the ball.
5. Supporting the man on the ball.
6. Penetration by blind side running.

3 v 4

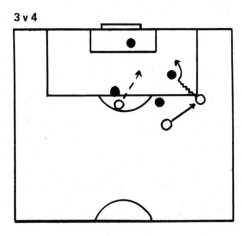

Points 1, 2 and 3

Often the wing player has time to use individual skill in a 1 v 1 situation. Deliberate encouragement of this ability should be incorporated in the function.

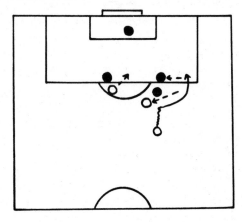

Points 4 and 5

In this case the link man decides to carry the ball forward while the winger attempts to destroy cover by running in front of two defenders and leaving space on the outside for the link man.

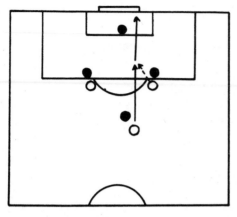

By switching the ball to the centre of the field, the defender may be caught turning. If the winger moves when he is on the "blind side" of the fullback, he can receive a penetrating through pass on the run.

The following possibilities might also be considered for practices:

1. Dribbling approaches to beat an opposing fullback.
2. Wall passing and through passing with an inside forward.
3. Fast run and centre from the wing.
4. Moving inside, away from touchline.
5. Making for the goal line and a low centre.
6. Lobbed centres and fast centres from various positions outside the penalty area.
7. Volley shooting and heading from centres from the other winger.
8. Tackling an opponent a second time.
9. Throw ins and corner kicks.
10. Ball control from services (all types) to be expected in a game.

Forwards

The primary function of forwards in soccer is to score goals. Apart from the skill practices covered in shooting and heading, players need to learn to recognize scoring opportunities. Too often forwards want to make an extra pass in tight situations, or simply want a clear shot on goal.

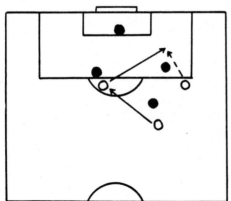

Use a practice of 3 against 4 attacking the goal to stress the basic principles of attempting to get a shot away at every opportunity in front of the penalty area. If the ball is forced out to the side, players should keep possession and look for support.

One forward may be selected for improvement in performance, and the opposition restricted initially in order to give him success. Eventually he will be exposed to the true situation, and all forwards should be aware of the following possibilities for recognizing and taking advantage of scoring situations.

Cut Back Ball

If one forward succeeds in taking the ball to the goal line, the supporting forwards should anticipate the ball being cut back by timing their run forward to arrive at full speed, not getting there too early to be covered in a static position.

Ball in the Air

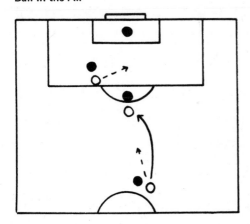

If the ball is played high to a marked forward, one attacker should go through, looking for a deflection, while the other supports from behind, looking for a poor clearance.

Destroying Cover

If the defence is set up with man-for-man marking, the two front forwards can open up the middle by intelligent running, leaving a 1 v 1 situation.

There are also many passing possibilities when man-for-man marking is employed, but forwards have to be coached in quick first time passing to take advantage of tight situations.

1. Shooting and heading situations near goal—a half chance taken when under careful marking by an opponent.
2. Attacking moves with inside forwards—three against two situations.
3. Moving to a wing position to receive a pass.
4. Ball control when marked by opponent.
5. Dealing with high clearances.
6. Use of setting up play to create space for other forwards.
7. Countering an offside plan.
8. Ball control and screening in a confined space.
9. Continuous running and checking to escape opponent's marking in order to receive pass.
10. Running on an opponent's blind side to receive pass. Making a pass to a third player running on opponent's blind side.
11. Throw ins, corner kicks, free kicks.

12
INDIVIDUAL PROGRAMS

INDIVIDUAL PROGRAMS FOR COACHES AND PLAYERS

Teaching Methods

The most expedient method of teaching physical education or games is for the coach to demonstrate the required skill and organize a suitable practice situation for the learners. This method presumes that the coach is capable of demonstrating accurately and that all learners will progress at the same rate.

The outline of lessons in this paper are adapted to the approach of individual programs in order to provide the coach who may not have the personal expertise with a prepared handout or lesson plan which players should follow to meet a required standard.

Lesson Plans and Individual Programs

The knowledgeable coach will be accustomed to plugging in the relevant drills and progressions to the lesson framework in order to improve upon the particular skills involved.

FRAMEWORK

Introductory Activities—10 Minutes

Warm-up activities should take the form of reviewing previously learned individual or pair activities and practicing of the skill items of the skill award program.

Main Theme—15 Minutes

Practice of linked skills utilizing the progressive teaching units as class lesson plans or allowing individuals to progress through the units at their own speed.

Related Games—10 Minutes

Utilization of learned skills in small sided game situations—see grid system.

PROGRAM

During the introductory session of the lesson, unit 1 will concentrate on the activities of the skill award program and participants should be encouraged to follow the practice activities outlined on the task sheet before attempting a standard. As improvement is made, however, they may keep track of their progress on the skill items and ask to be evaluated when they can achieve a standard, or the teacher may have an evaluation session. The use of stations in various locations of the activity area is particularly useful in accommodating large groups.

SKILL AWARD PROGRAM

The development of skill and motivation to practice skills has been of concern to coaches at all levels of the game in order to provide an incentive for competence in basic skills.

A soccer skill awards program has been developed, i.e., specific standards for Bronze, Silver and Gold crests in each age group from 7 to 17 years of age. There are six test items which can be practiced as training activities and tested when a player feels he can achieve a specific crest.

In this way each individual will receive recognition for his efforts and will have continuing incentive to achieve a standard at each successive age level.

A skills contest could be sponsored by selecting the gold award candidates of any age group for a final competition or annual awards could be made to the highest standard achieved in each age group. In addition, an award could be made to the "most skillful team" by awarding points for each award attained by the members of a youth soccer team. For example:

Gold—3 points
Silver—2 points
Bronze—1 point

The concept has many applications but the most important application is to the improvement of the players themselves.

The skill awards should provide an incentive for youth soccer players to practice the individual skills of the game and to attract newcomers.

SKILL AWARD PROGRAM

Crests will be Awarded on the
Basis of the Level of Achievement

INDIVIDUAL PRACTICE—JUGGLING

INDIVIDUAL SKILLS CREST

1. Drop ball from hands and allow it to bounce. Strike ball once with instep (laced area of shoe) and allow to bounce again.
2. Keep toe back to make ball go straight up in air and just above head height.
3. Use left foot, then right foot, with one bounce of the ball on the ground in between.
4. Try to use left foot, then right, with no bounce in between.
5. Try two bounces on left foot, with a bounce in between, then two bounces on right foot with a bounce in between.
6. Practice until you can keep the ball up for 2, 3 and 4 touches until you reach your own personal best.
7. Use your thigh or upper leg for juggling by dropping the ball from hands to make one, two, three, etc., contacts with the ball before losing control.
8. Remember, contact the ball when your thigh is flat under the ball, not at an angle. Try for your record.
9. Start with your thigh again and, if you lose control, try to bring the ball back to thigh level with your instep.
10. Use your insteps and thighs to keep the ball in the air as long as you can. Try to beat your record.

Test

Look at the standards for juggling in the skill award booklet and try to achieve a level for your age group. To improve your score, work at the practices before being tested again.

Teaching Aids:

Pelé poster on juggling
Pelé film on juggling

Personal Progress Chart and Results

Select a level for each test item (on your own or with the help of a coach). Enter these in your "Personal Progress Chart." Test yourself as often as possible, recording your best scores on the chart. When you have reached your first goal, it's time to select a new one. When you achieve an award standard, send in the results.

LEVEL/AGE	7	8	9	10	11	12	13	14	15	16	17
Bronze	4	5	8	10	12	13	15	16	17	18	20
Silver	7	8	10	12	15	16	20	21	22	23	25
Gold	10	10	12	15	20	30	45	50	60	60	60

1 Juggling

Description: Keeping the ball in the air using all parts of the body. Player is allowed the best of two attempts.

Scoring: Number of contacts in air.

Skill Development: Balance, agility, reaction and "feel" for the ball.

Name	Age	Juggling	Award

SKILL AWARD PROGRAM

Crests will be Awarded on the
Basis of the Level of Achievement

INDIVIDUAL PRACTICE—HEAD JUGGLING

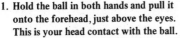

INDIVIDUAL SKILLS CREST

1. Hold the ball in both hands and pull it onto the forehead, just above the eyes. This is your head contact with the ball.
2. Tilt your head back until the forehead is under the ball and you are looking straight up (one foot in front of the other will help your balance).
3. Throw the ball up, contact once with forehead, and catch.
4. Try two bounces on the head, and catch.
5. Try to move under the ball as you attempt your personal best.
6. Remember to head the ball upwards and not forward by moving under the "drop" of the ball each time you contact it.

Heading Games

1. Throw ball up against wall and head the rebound back against the wall. Remember to keep your eyes open and contact it with the forehead.

2. Try to continue heading the rebound from the wall as often as possible to develop timing and power in your heading.
3. Pick a partner who is practicing heading and try to keep the ball up in the air between you by striking it one after the other with the forehead.

Test

Look at the standards for head juggling in the skill award booklet and try to achieve a level for your age group. To improve, work at the practices before being tested again.

Teaching Aids:

Pelé poster on heading
Pelé film on heading (16 mm)
Film loop on basic headings (8 mm)
(*Encyclopaedia Britannica*)

Personal Progress Chart and Results

Select a level for each test item (on your own or with the help of a coach). Enter these in your "Personal Progress Chart." Test yourself as often as possible, recording your best scores on the chart. When you have reached your first goal, it's time to select a new one. When you achieve an award standard, send in the results.

LEVEL/AGE	7	8	9	10	11	12	13	14	15	16	17
Bronze	4	4	6	7	8	9	10	11	12	13	15
Silver	5	6	7	8	9	10	12	13	14	15	20
Gold	7	8	9	10	11	12	13	14	15	20	30

2 Head Juggling

Description: Keeping the ball in the air using the head only. Player is allowed the best of two attempts.

Scoring: Total number of contacts.

Skill Development: Balance, agility, reaction and "feel" for the ball.

Name	Age	Head Juggling	Award

SKILL AWARD PROGRAM

Crests will be Awarded on the Basis of the Level of Achievement

INDIVIDUAL PRACTICE—RUNNING

INDIVIDUAL SKILLS CREST

Build up your stamina for the 300 yard run by running "repeats" of shorter distances. For example:

1. Run across the gym and touch each wall. Make five trips as quickly as possible. Rest for 30 seconds, then repeat until you can do this 3 times at full speed.

   On the soccer field, sprint from the goal line to the edge of the 18 yard box and back 3 times, rest, and repeat twice more.

2. Touch wall at each *end* of the gym, making three trips as quickly as possible. Rest

for 30 seconds, then repeat once more.

On the soccer field, sprint *across* the width of the penalty box 4 times, rest, and repeat once more.

Test

Time yourself on the 300 yard run outlined in the skill award program, and look up the standards for your age group. If you wish to improve your time, try to improve your speed on the *practices* before trying the test again.

Personal Progress Chart and Results

Select a level for each test item (on your own or with the help of a coach). Enter these in your "Personal Progress Chart." Test yourself as often as possible, recording your best scores on the chart. When you have reached your first goal, it's time to select a new one. When you achieve an award standard, send in the results.

LEVEL/AGE	7	8	9	10	11	12	13	14	15	16	17
Bronze	88	82	77	74	71	68	65	62	59	58	56
Silver	78	74	70	67	65	63	60	57	55	54	53
Gold	73	69	66	64	60	59	58	56	52	51	50

3 300 Yard Run

Description: Run a 100 yard course from the start to a 50 yard marker and return, three times.

Scoring: Use a stopwatch to time from the starting signal until the runner crosses the finish line.

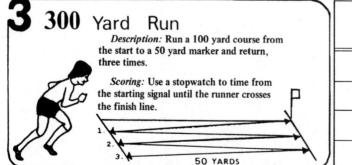

50 YARDS

Name	Age	300 Yard Run	Award

SKILL AWARD PROGRAM

Crests will be Awarded on the Basis of the Level of Achievement

INDIVIDUAL PRACTICE—SHUTTLE RUN

INDIVIDUAL SKILLS CREST

1. Practice running with the ball at speed, then stopping it with the sole of your foot, right and left.
2. Contact the ball with the outside of your foot every stride over 10 yards.
3. Practice checking and going in the opposite direction by stopping the ball behind a line and sprinting back where you started from with the ball.

group. To improve, work on the practices before being tested again.

Teaching Aids:

Pelé poster on dribbling
Pelé film on dribbling (16 mm)
Film loop on running with ball (8 mm)
(*Encyclopaedia Britannica*)

Test

Try the test item in the skill award program and check the time standard for your age

Personal Progress Chart and Results

Select a level for each test item (on your own or with the help of a coach). Enter these in your "Personal Progress Chart." Test yourself as often as possible, recording your best scores on the chart. When you have reached your first goal, it's time to select a new one. When you achieve an award standard, send in the results.

LEVEL/AGE	7	8	9	10	11	12	13	14	15	16	17
Bronze	20.0	19.0	18.0	17.0	16.0	15.8	15.5	15.0	14.5	14.0	13.0
Silver		19.0	17.0	16.0	15.0	14.8	14.6	14.5	14.0	13.5	13.0	12.5
Gold		18.0	16.0	15.0	14.5	14.0	13.5	13.0	12.5	12.0	11.5	11.0

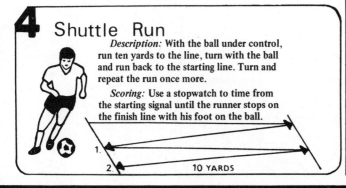

4 Shuttle Run

Description: With the ball under control, run ten yards to the line, turn with the ball and run back to the starting line. Turn and repeat the run once more.

Scoring: Use a stopwatch to time from the starting signal until the runner stops on the finish line with his foot on the ball.

1.
2.   10 YARDS

Name	Age	Shuttle Run	Award

SKILL AWARD PROGRAM

Crests will be Awarded on the
Basis of the Level of Achievement

INDIVIDUAL PRACTICE—DRIBBLING

INDIVIDUAL SKILLS CREST

1. Practice running with the ball under close control. Use inside, outside and sole of both feet.
2. Work in a confined space where others are practicing the same skill, trying to avoid contact and losing your ball.
3. Dribble the ball along a line, and weave from side to side of the line without losing control. Try to stay as close to the line as possible.

Test

Practice the test item until you can weave through the cones with control before speeding up to record your best time. To improve, work on the practices and the test drill.

Teaching Aids:

The same as for the shuttle run.

Personal Progress Chart and Results

Select a level for each test item (on your own or with the help of a coach). Enter these in your "Personal Progress Chart." Test yourself as often as possible, recording your best scores on the chart. When you have reached your first goal, it's time to select a new one. When you achieve an award standard, send in the results.

LEVEL/AGE	7	8	9	10	11	12	13	14	15	16	17
Bronze	20.0	19.0	18.5	18.0	17.5	17.0	16.5	16.0	15.5	15.0	14.5
Silver	18.0	17.0	16.5	16.0	15.5	15.0	14.5	14.0	13.5	13.0	12.5
Gold	15.5	15.0	14.5	14.0	13.8	13.5	13.2	13.0	12.5	12.0	11.5

5 Dribbling

Description: Set up six cones or markers two yards apart over a distance of ten yards. The player begins with the ball at his feet at the first marker and weaves in and out of the markers in a zigzag fashion around the end marker and back to the starting point.

Scoring: Use a stopwatch to time from the starting signal until the runner stops at the last cone with his foot on the ball.

◄——— 10 YARDS ———►

Name	Age	Dribbling	Award

INDIVIDUAL PRACTICE—
WALL VOLLEY

Find a suitable stretch of gym wall (indoor or out) or work with a teammate and try the following practices:

1. Practice inside of foot technique with ball stationary:
   —step up to the ball
   —contact with inside of foot turned flat to meet ball (slapping)
   —swing your lower leg through after the ball
   —ask for unit 2 technique practice for inside of foot pass
2. Practice returning the ball first time (without stopping it) to a teammate or rebounding off the wall. Build up to make as many returns as possible without losing control. Remember to lift your foot slightly to contact the centre of the ball.
3. Practice getting behind the ball as it comes to you to play it first time or control if it is bouncing awkwardly before using the inside of your foot again. (See unit on receiving.)

Test

When you can consistently return the ball without stopping, try the test item to record your score within the time limits. To improve, work on improving technique with the inside of your foot and instep. (See unit on instep drive.)

6 Wall Volley

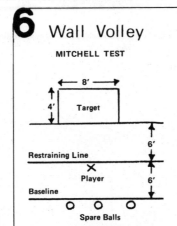

MITCHELL TEST

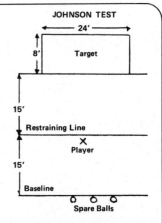

JOHNSON TEST

Description: Two wall volley tests are described: the Mitchell Wall Volley Test (1) for players up to 12 years of age and the Johnson Wall Volley Test (2) for players from 13 to 17 years of age.

Wall Volley tests are excellent training and conditioning aids, particularly indoors during the winter. These wall volley tests were developed as a single item test to measure soccer skill and they have been found to correlate closely with a player's skill during a game.

Mark out the indicated dimensions on a gymnasium or suitable wall area with tape, chalk or paint.

Description:
1. On command *go*, start test immediately. Drop the ball—it need not bounce before you play it against

the target area. Continue to play ball to target area until the command *stop*.
2. You may use any skills. Play ball from behind line.
3. You may cross line to retrieve ball, but hits won't count. Use spare balls, if necessary, to save time.
4. Each ball striking the wall in the marked area and returning over the restraining line before *stop* counts as a hit and scores one point.
5. Three trials—total score.

Scoring:
Johnson Test: Three 30 second attempts—total score.
Mitchell Test: Three 20 second attempts—total score.

(1) Mitchell, Reid, "A Wall-Volley Test for Measuring Soccer Ability in Fifth and Sixth Grade Boys." Unpublished Master's Thesis, University of Oregon, 1963.

(2) Johnson, Joseph Robert, "The Development of a single item test as a measure of Soccer Skill." Master's Thesis, University of British Columbia, 1963.

Personal Progress Chart and Results

Select a level for each test item (on your own or with the help of a coach). Enter these in your "Personal Progress Chart." Test yourself as often as possible, recording your best scores on the chart. When you have reached your first goal, it's time to select a new one. When you achieve an award standard, send in the results.

LEVEL/AGE	7	8	9	10	11	12	13	14	15	16	17
Bronze	13	14	15	16	17	18	26	27	28	29	30
Silver	20	21	22	23	24	25	33	34	35	36	37
Gold	25	26	27	28	29	30	38	39	40	41	42

Name	Age	Wall Volley	Award

SOCCER SCHOOL AWARD PROGRAM

ORDER FORM C.1.

SKILL AWARD	NUMBER
Juggling	
Heading	
Fitness	
Shuttle Run	
Dribbling	
Passing & Shooting	
TOTAL NO.	

ORDER FORM C.2.

ACHIEVEMENT LEVEL			
Gold	Silver	Bronze	Participation

TOTAL No.

SHIP TO/ENVOYER À

Name/Nom _____

Address/Adresse _____

City/Ville _____

Prov. _____

SOCCER 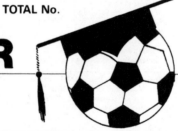 SCHOOL

MAIL TO:
THE SOCCER SCHOOL
Box 6087, Station J
Ottawa, Ontario K2A 1T1, Canada

Code No.	Quantity	Description	Bulk Price	Unit Price	Total
B.10		Soccer School	10 for $20.00	3.50	
B.11		Soccer Coaching Methods	5 for $40.00	9.00	
B.12		Teaching Soccer	5 for $40.00	9.00	
C.1		Skill Crests (Individual)	100 for $45.00	50¢	
C.2		Achievement Levels	100 for $45.00	50¢	
F.		Soccer School Film (16 mm)		$60.00	
K.1		Principles of Play Slides		$40.00 per set	
K.2		Systems of Play Slides		$60.00 per set	
		Poster of Award Program	10 for $2.50	50¢	

Total _____

Postage/Handling Charge — Orders under $15.00 — $2.00
Orders over $15.00 — $3.00

GRAND TOTAL _____
(Cheque enclosed)

The Soccer School reserves the right to invoice at costs prevailing at time of dispatch.

To: SOCCER PUBLICATIONS, INC. $8.95

    3530 Greer Road
    Palo Alto, California 94303

Please send me _____ copies of **SOCCER COACHING METHODS**. Enclosed
is my check or money order for $_____ which includes the price of
$8.95 per book plus $1.50 for the first book ($.50 for each additional book)
for shipping and handling. (California residents add 6% sales tax).

NAME _____

ADDRESS _____

CITY,STATE,ZIP _____

ORGANIZATION _____

GROUP DISCOUNTS ARE AVAILABLE...CALL (415)494-6338.

To: SOCCER PUBLICATIONS, INC. $8.95

    3530 Greer Road
    Palo Alto, California 94303

Please send me _____ copies of **SOCCER COACHING METHODS**. Enclosed
is my check or money order for $_____ which includes the price of
$8.95 per book plus $1.50 for the first book ($.50 for each additional book)
for shipping and handling. (California residents add 6% sales tax).

NAME _____

ADDRESS _____

CITY,STATE,ZIP _____

ORGANIZATION _____

GROUP DISCOUNTS ARE AVAILABLE...CALL (415)494-6338.

Please enclose this card with your payment and
send to:

SOCCER PUBLICATIONS, INC.
3530 Greer Road
Palo Alto, California 94303

Please enclose this card with your payment and
send to:

SOCCER PUBLICATIONS, INC.
3530 Greer Road
Palo Alto, California 94303